Bad Dog
to
Best Friend

The Transformation

of

Dakota

Non-Fiction — Aliens

Ancient Aliens and the Lost Islands: Through the Wormhole
Ancient Aliens and the Age of Giants: Through the Wormhole
Alien Nightmares: Screen Memories of UFO Alien Abductions

Non-Fiction — Nature

An Acre of America Backyard Nature Series:
The Wizard of Awe
Over the Hummingbird's Rainbow
King of the Forest

Audubon: The Dream That Wouldn't Die
plus the Back Yard Nature Kids series by Della Rose

Non-Fiction — Other

Bad Dog to Best Friend
Training Your Dog to be Home Alone
Yankee, Go Home
Wedding Anniversary Gifts for Coin Collectors
Insider Secrets for a Successful Website Business
666 and the IRS: Taxes are the Work of the Devil
Ten Dead Mice: See How They Died

Fiction

Fomorian Earth: Star Borne: 1
Shades of Moloch: Star Borne: 2
Renegade Genius: Star Borne: 3
The Cantor Dimension: An Astrophysical Murder Mystery

Audiobooks & Blog

T-shirt & Gift Shop

Bad Dog to Best Friend

There's hope for even the worst dog

The Transformation of Dakota

by Sharon Delarose

GITYASOME BOOKS - A DIVISION OF GYPSY KING SOFTWARE

No part of this book may be reproduced, scanned, distributed, or transmitted
in any electronic or printed form, including photocopying, recording,
and all other information storage and retrieval systems,
without written permission from the author, except in the case of
brief quotations embodied in articles written as book reviews.
Thank you!

This book is based on the true story of Dakota.

Published by Gityasome Books
a division of Gypsy King Software, Inc.
www.sharondelarose.com

Printed in the United States of America
Second Edition

ISBN: 1453683178
EAN-13: 9781453683170

Dedicated to my husband Bear
who encouraged me to share Dakota's story,

and

to Gypsy Rose, the first dog I adopted from a dog pound.
Gypsy Rose taught me that used dogs aren't always bad dogs and
that sometimes the best dogs come from the dog pound.

Acknowledgements

To the thousands of dog pounds and dog rescue groups who take in society's unwanted dogs: I hope Dakota's story will teach people how to keep their dogs instead of abandoning them to their deaths.

To Victoria Stilwell: Thank you for bringing your decades of experience with training dogs and their owners to the television channel Animal Planet. I highly recommend the television show *It's Me or the Dog* to anyone with a dog.

To James Herriot, author of *All Creatures Great and Small:* Thank you for so vividly describing the personalities of the many dogs you encountered.

There is no better way to understand your dog than to read the many stories of James Herriot — not just his dog books, but all of his books are full of insight into the world of dogs.

To the Monks of New Skete, authors of *How to Be Your Dog's Best Friend*: Thank you for sharing techniques such as keeping a dog-in-training on a leash, even in the house. So simple and so effective! For those who've never heard of the monks, they've been training dogs for decades and share their wisdom through books and videos.

To Karen Ackerman, my lifelong friend: Without your insight into the subtleties of the concept of alpha dog and other tidbits of dog wisdom, I never would have adopted a dog. You showed me that all it takes to have a good dog, is to be a good teacher.

Contents

Before Dakota — There Was Gypsy Rose

We often hesitate to adopt a dog from the dog pound because we don't know what we're getting into when we adopt somebody else's used dog. We assume that if the dog is at the pound there must be a reason. He chews up your smelly shoes, pees on Aunt Molly, or rummages through the trash. There must be something really wrong for the dog to be at the pound.

That's the big myth. In fact, when you adopt a dog from a shelter they often have a record about the dog, including any training he's had and whether he's been an indoor or outdoor dog. They've spent a few days around him and know if he's friendly, aggressive, fearful, etc. Dogs don't just appear on their doorstep — the owners turn them in and are required to fill out a fact sheet about the dog.

We adopted Gypsy Rose from the Humane Society. According to their records Gypsy Rose was housebroken, knew the command sit, and preferred the outdoors. I liked what I saw in her eyes — they were calm. She wasn't jumping around and barking like the other dogs. There was no sign of aggression or fear in her. She didn't growl or cower in a corner. She sat calmly, looking at me with a question mark in her eyes.

After adopting her it didn't take long for me to realize that Gypsy Rose was very well-trained. She knew several commands, was quiet, and she was totally trustworthy when left alone in the house. I could not understand how Gypsy Rose came to be abandoned by two different families. Somebody, somewhere, had spent a lot of time training her and it showed.

Gypsy Rose was about the closest thing to the perfect dog that I ever could have imagined and it baffled me utterly that anyone would have gotten rid of her. To think how close she was to the gas chamber brings tears to my eyes even now. She'd been at the dog pound for a week already and I don't know how long they keep a dog before the axe falls, but I don't think it's much more than a week.

In addition to being well-trained, Gypsy Rose was an incredibly good natured dog. We took her on countless road trips with us. She was a great traveler, and our friends and family welcomed her into their homes for a visit. She was that good, and she came to us that way.

Then came Dakota — the Dog from Hell

After our good fortune in finding such a well-trained dog the first time around, we didn't hesitate to take a chance adopting another used dog. Unfortunately, we were not as lucky the second time around.

Dakota had so many problems that most people would have taken her back to the shelter, where she surely would have been killed. Our first weeks with Dakota brought us nothing but misery. She peed all over the house, destroyed her food bowl and automatic water dispenser, chewed up blankets, dumped incredible quantities of poop and smeared it on everything in her reach including herself. She barked all day and disturbed the neighbors, bullied Gypsy Rose, didn't know even the most basic commands — and she was a wild child.

We hadn't anticipated the level of commitment that Dakota needed in order to retrain her, and neither of us had the experience of retraining a dog who someone else had so badly mishandled. In addition, we discovered that the quirks of her particular breed added challenges of their own to her training, making it even more difficult.

In spite of our lack of experience and the severity of her problems, we embarked on an incredible journey of discovery with Dakota. She amazed us with her intelligence and desire to learn new things. Most of all she brought incredible joy and laughter into our lives.

However, our journey with Dakota was not a smooth one. We stumbled over her stubborn and independent nature. She was scrappy and resourceful like a rebellious, streetwise teenager that had been shuffled from foster home to foster home, unwanted and unloved. It took a long time for Dakota to open up and trust us. In addition, she was the Master of Dirty Tricks. She was ready for us, but we weren't ready for her.

It was a bumpy road but under our care and guidance, Dakota was transformed into a dog who could be left home alone for many hours without pottying or chewing us out of house and home. She became a dog who we trusted enough to take on road trips. Dakota became our best friend and beloved companion. Today I cannot imagine a life without her in it. We would have missed out on so much love, laughter, and joy had we not taken the time to retrain her.

This is the story of Dakota's transformation from the most godawful dog imaginable, to the best friend we could ever hope to share our home with. Our trials and tribulations in training her, every technique we used, both the successes and the failures, we offer in the hopes of helping other dog owners.

There is hope for even the worst dog. May your journeys take you to a place of love and laughter with your dog, as ours have.

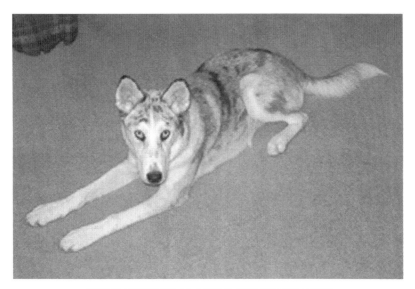

SHE CAME TO US AS A WILD AND BRATTY DOG

Meet Dakota — The Dog from Hell

Dakota didn't come to us as well-behaved as Gypsy Rose, the previous dog we'd adopted from the dog pound. Adult dogs, especially those who've been abandoned by their owners, have unique needs.

Dakota was seven months old, and she was what they call a yo-yo dog, having been shuffled from place-to-place her entire life. Within days of adopting her we understood why her previous owners had sent her packing.

Dakota was a problem child. She peed all over the house, she bullied our other dog, and she barked non-stop when we went to work. She was wild and out of control because she hadn't been taught even the most basic of commands. In addition, she was destructive. She wanted to chew anything that came into her sphere because nobody had taken the time to teach her not to.

For reasons I can't explain, we chose to commit ourselves to this wild child. Under our guidance Dakota was transformed into a quiet dog who could be trusted home alone for hours without pottying, barking, or tearing up the house. This is her story, and the techniques we used to retrain her.

Adoption Day

The decision to adopt a second dog
(What the dog experts would have told us had we asked)

We did not set out to adopt a dog that day. Our other dog was elderly and we had been debating the issue of when to adopt again. Do we adopt another dog while we still have Gypsy Rose? Do we wait until she passes away?

Our assumptions:

(1) Gypsy Rose, the perfect dog, could help us train a new dog to be perfect.

(2) The new dog would be good company for Gypsy Rose, who enjoyed being around other dogs.

(3) Gypsy Rose would regain a bit of her youth if she had a younger dog to play with.

(4) We could avoid potty training by adopting a dog that was already housebroken, allowing us to build on the fundamentals of training rather than start from scratch.

(5) It would be easier for us to adjust to a new dog if we were emotionally invested in the new dog before Gypsy Rose passed away.

Gypsy Rose — a shelter dog who had come to us at a year and a half old being already trained, housebroken, trustworthy, quiet, and eager to please — had spoiled us. We were hoping to repeat the positive experience.

As we debated the issue of when to adopt again, we put out a few feelers. We had visited the dog pound a couple of times and none of the dogs appealed to us. A dog is a lifelong commitment and we needed to feel comfortable with our choice. Although we hadn't made the decision to adopt yet, we did tend to gravitate toward dogs looking for homes. The official adoption day grabbed us without warning. We went to the pet store to buy dog food and they were hosting Pet Adoption Day in conjunction with a local animal shelter.

Immediately we were drawn to Dakota. We'd always loved the idea of having a Siberian Husky. Dakota's coloring was very Husky-like and yet her hair was short. After battling Gypsy Rose's long hair for many years, short hair was appealing. They told us she was an Australian Cattle Dog mix and it was obvious that the other half was Siberian Husky.

Dakota was calm, even during the test walk, and her eyes shined with intelligence. They told us that she was housebroken, crate trained, and good with other dogs. Add to that her very striking coloring, and we were hooked.

We adopted Dakota on the spot and took her into the pet store for food bowls, a collar and a leash. A lady customer came up to us and said, "Isn't that the dog from the dog pound? I saw her there with her sister and boy, did she look like a handful!" The warning she'd given was well deserved and to this day, I wonder if that lady was her previous owner, hanging in the background to see the fate of her unwanted dog. I later discovered that the shelter hosting Dakota didn't allow visitors on site so the lady couldn't possibly have seen her at the dog pound, reinforcing my theory that she'd been the one to dump Dakota at the shelter.

As for our assumptions, only one of them turned out to be correct. Adopting Dakota did not bring joy and companionship to Gypsy Rose as we'd hoped. In fact, it brought her nothing but misery. Training Dakota turned out to be a major undertaking due to the bad habits she'd already established. The only thing we'd actually accomplished was to ease our own transition to a new dog when Gypsy Rose finally did pass away.

Did they say housebroken?
(Also known as Grab Your Mop)

Our house is carpeted — almost every inch of it. We didn't have a regular room to put a new dog in that wasn't carpeted, nor did we have a fenced yard. That left the garage, a small bathroom, or a carpeted room. As she was destined to become an indoor dog, we brought Dakota immediately into the house. After all, they told us she was housebroken so it should have been safe to bring her indoors.

The first thing Dakota did in the house was to squat and pee. I hauled out the carpet shampooer — thankfully we had one — and shampooed the spot immediately. Then I sprayed it with a 50-50 vinegar/water solution.

Treating the area with a vinegar solution is supposed to prevent the dog from going back to that spot to pee. It doesn't, however, prevent them from peeing somewhere else. Before I could finish cleaning the first mess, Dakota squatted and peed again. This went on for the first two hours. We were off to a jolly good start — so much for being housebroken.

Dakota was what they call a yo-yo dog, shuffled from home to home until she met us. She'd been at the dog pound twice, in addition to two other places that we knew of. We were her fifth home in seven months including her stints at the dog pound.

She had no idea who we were, what had happened to her old home, or what to expect from us. Dakota was highly stressed and we were careful not to immediately come down on her and stress her out even more. In addition, Dakota came to us malnourished. Her rib bones were sticking out pretty noticeably. As she'd only been at the dog pound for a couple of days it was obvious that they weren't at fault. Her previous owners had failed to feed her enough. Dakota had some serious issues with trusting people. In her short life people had not been very good to her.

Focus on her good qualities
(Amid chaos, there is hope… Amid hope, there is chaos)

Amid the chaos we saw hope. In spite of her rocky beginnings with us, Dakota showed some very good signs. She slept through the night loose in our bedroom without peeing and without bothering Gypsy Rose. At mealtimes we were able to approach her even while she was eating, and Dakota was not aggressive. Even with her history of not getting enough food, she did not warn us away.

In addition, Dakota was a quiet dog. She did not bark when we were sleeping, and she did not bark at every movement she saw out the window. In fact, we had to teach her to bark when someone came to the door. Most of all, Dakota was eager to learn. These were very good signs.

Another good sign was when I gave her a bath outdoors the day after adopting her. She was smelly with god knows what and we didn't want her smearing it all over the house, so we decided that a bath was imminent. Dakota was pretty calm about the whole thing even though she clearly didn't like it. Here I was, a total stranger, giving her a bath, and she was being pretty good about it — very good signs indeed.

Remember — we weren't prepared for her, we hadn't set out to adopt a dog that day, and we were winging it. Three days after adopting her, we had to go to work. What were we going to do with Dakota?

She wasn't ready to be left loose in the house. We didn't even trust her enough to confine her to a single room, and we hadn't gotten a crate for her, never having used one before. That left the garage. We confined Dakota to a portion of the garage and off we went for the day. We anticipated that she'd potty in the garage so we put down some paper in case she'd been paper trained and we left her with food and water.

My husband got home first. Nothing could have prepared him for what he walked into. Dakota had pooped everywhere. Not only had she pooped, she had managed to smear it all over herself, the floor, the food bowl, the water dispenser, and all of the toys we'd left for her. Welcome Home!

Don't Kill the Dog

Potty training a yo-yo dog is a challenging task. They are highly stressed from being bounced from home to home and they live in fear of being abandoned again. What does a stressed dog do? It pees.

Dakota had the secondary problem of being a nervous pee-er. If she was stressed, she peed. If she was excited, she peed. If you raised your voice one iota, she peed. If she was mad at you, she peed. If the urge struck, she peed. While putting the leash on to take her out to pee, she peed — every time.

Our first weeks with Dakota were a nightmare of hauling out the carpet shampooer and scrubbing the garage floor over and over again. We hadn't expected this level of commitment having been told she was already housebroken. You'd think that the days she spent in the garage would be easier, but they were actually harder and a lot more work than the carpet shampooer.

Dakota dumped incredible quantities of poop when she was in the garage and she smeared it everywhere. Every single thing in her reach would be covered with poop by the time we got home from work, including Dakota herself. Amazingly she did not do this in the house, only the garage. Maybe the cement floor of the garage felt like a dog pound to her. Maybe not being in the house where her comfort zone was stressed her out. Who knew?

In addition, Dakota barked all day according to the neighbors. Even from the garage they could hear her two houses away, and she destroyed her water bowl. We hadn't put her good water bowl in the garage with her. Instead we left her with a butter bowl full of water on our workdays. As soon as we were out of sight she tipped the bowl over and proceeded to chew the butter bowl into a million little pieces. Everything we tried to do for her was a tug of war. We tried to do something good for her and Dakota turned it into a nightmare.

Don't kill the dog
(That wild bucking bronco wallowing in dog poop)

My commute to work is an hour and a half each way so after working all day and then battling traffic, I'd come home to Dakota and the alien world she'd created in the garage with everything smeared in poop. Every evening before I could relax, I had to scrub down the garage floor with a long handled scrubber and hose, and then hand wash every single thing that had been within her reach. Dried dog poop on a concrete floor doesn't come off easily. It turns into a super-glued cement and no amount of scrubbing will completely remove it. At least after that first day she hadn't smeared herself with poop again which was a small consolation during those hours of unexpected garage duty.

I have no doubt whatsoever that if anybody else had adopted Dakota, she'd have quickly ended up right back at the dog pound. There aren't many people willing to commit themselves the way we had to commit to Dakota. We were utterly miserable but we were also determined. I knew what Dakota's ultimate fate would be if we failed her, and it wasn't a good one. Besides, Dakota was actually great fun. She had a unique personality and you couldn't help but love her. In her good moments she was utterly charming and she made us laugh a lot.

You have to see this from Dakota's point of view. Most people don't see it from a dog's perspective and that truly helps in training your dog and understanding them. Dakota had been bounced from home to home for seven months, she had been at the dog pound twice, and we were total strangers to her. She'd only been with us a few days when we left her in the garage. She had no way of knowing that this was part of her new home and not a dog pound. She had no idea if we were coming back or if this was another abandonment. She had no reason to trust us. Everybody else who had passed through her life had let her down. Dakota had to learn to trust in her new family unit and this would take time.

So off I'd go to work leaving my husband a sticky note: *"Don't kill the dog!"* Being the first one home he had to encounter this wild-eyed bucking bronco who was literally mad with frenzy. He had to traverse a veritable minefield of puddles and poop to put a leash on her, and then somehow maneuver this frantic dog through the minefield and out into the yard without getting jumped on with potty feet.

The clean-up was my job and I spent an hour every evening scrubbing, hosing, washing toys, bones, and other dog paraphernalia. Dakota was a lot of work those first weeks.

Dakota's Trip to Misery

What had we done to her?
(Our dog hung her head in abject misery and I cried)

Five weeks after we adopted Dakota, we went out of town for a week and boarded her. Normally we don't board our dogs. We either take them with us, or we find a local helper to come to our home and care for the dogs, but Dakota was such a nightmare that we couldn't do either one, so off she went to the boarding kennel.

She arrived at the kennel with head high and tail wagging, enthusiastically awaiting this new adventure. Dakota was a happy dog. We'd plucked her from the dog pound and a life of revolving doors and brought her into a place of abundance. Even when she was in trouble she was happy, and we had dubbed her *Dakota the Undauntable*. She enjoyed her newfound home and family and even if we were mad at her, Dakota didn't mind it.

She lived in the house with us in comfort, she had another dog to torment, and we provided plenty of food and water unlike her previous home. She also had toys to play with, bones to chew on, and people who loved her and played games with her. For Dakota, life was very, very good.

Gypsy Rose went on the great adventure with us — the adventure being a road trip of several hundred miles. We waved goodbye to Dakota and off we went for a week. I agonized the entire time. I could not relax and enjoy the trip for worrying over Dakota. I hated to board her knowing that the boarding kennel would feel like another dog pound abandonment, but there wasn't much I could have done differently — or so I thought.

ME AND GYPSY ROSE ON THE ROAD TRIP

After the trip we went to collect Dakota from the dog kennel. The change in her was so profound that I cried. Dakota's head was hanging low in abject misery, her tail was tucked between her legs and she was shaking badly. Dakota's entire demeanor was that of a dog who'd been totally beaten down. She hadn't seen us yet and she looked utterly destroyed. She absolutely thought she'd been abandoned again and for Dakota, the week had obviously been pure and utter hell.

Our happy dog had morphed into the most miserable dog you could imagine. On top of that she came back to us literally crawling with both fleas and worms, transmitting both to our other dog. Now we had two flea-bitten dogs going mad with itching and our flea treatments weren't working. Every night I had a new job in addition to the scrubbing of the garage: picking fleas off the dogs.

I tormented myself over what we'd done to Dakota by boarding her. What could we have done differently? I soon found the answer. We got Dakota a dog crate. If we'd had the crate before the trip she could have come with us. It would have been far better for her to be with us even if she had to spend much of her time in the crate. Either way she was in a cage, right? She would not have felt abandoned, she would not have gotten fleas and worms, and we all would have been much happier.

The dog crate
(Gift from the Gods)

I'm not a big fan of locking a dog in a box. Gypsy Rose had full run of the house and she was a dreamboat, but Dakota was a long way from dreamboat status and we needed tools to deal with her special needs. The crate opened up a whole new world and for Dakota, this was a positive change. The dog crate allowed Dakota to stay in the house when we were at work. This was more in her comfort zone. Gypsy Rose was close by and Dakota could see and smell her new home so she wasn't as panicky. Dakota didn't feel the abandonment fear that the garage left her with. Being in a crate in the house didn't feel like a dog pound.

We purchased a large crate for her not knowing how big she'd get and wanting to be able to use it when we traveled with her. In spite of all her problems, we had hopes of eventually taking her on road trips with us. Our dog crate had a divider so you could make it smaller inside if it was too big for the dog. It also had doors on three sides and folded into a suitcase. The dog crate fit perfectly in the back seat of the truck which had seats that folded down flat, and having a door on each end allowed us to let Dakota in and out without taking the crate out of the truck. It was the perfect setup for road trips. In addition, the crate was big enough to comfortably fit both dogs, and the divider would keep Dakota from bullying Gypsy Rose.

The dog crate was a pivotal moment in Dakota's progress. She did not potty in the crate — she actually held it all day long on our workdays. No more did I have to spend an hour scrubbing down the garage every night. Not only that, once we brought her indoors on our workdays, Dakota stopped barking. The crate allowed her to be in the house which put her into a comfort zone. The garage was just too much like the dog pound. Indoors Dakota was happier, more at peace, and we had a solution for our next road trip.

Potty Training a Problem Dog

One problem solved, many more to go
(Adrift in a sea of dog pee, I saw a glimmer of hope)

Now that we'd solved the workday problem we were back to Dakota's bad habit of peeing in the house when she wasn't in the crate — which was anytime we were home with her. Dakota didn't give a lot of warning before she peed. She didn't sniff or circle looking for the perfect place. She simply stopped in midstride, squatted and peed all in about one second. Dakota was that quick.

We trained her to pee outdoors by using food as a bribe. Dakota had an insatiable craving for food and we used this in her training. We bought a bag of large kibble dog food different from her normal food. Every time she peed outdoors we gave her a piece of food as a reward. You'd think it was a hunk of steak the way she coveted that potty treat and she quickly learned to pee outdoors. The trouble was — she still peed indoors. No matter how often we took her out, we couldn't seem to stop her from peeing indoors. It seemed hopeless.

I'LL TRY TO BE A GOOD DOG, I PROMISE!

We chose to embrace positive dog training techniques as much as possible, which means training with a reward system instead of a fear system, so we tried to focus on the potty treats. We made it clear to her that we were not pleased when she peed indoors, but we had to be very careful in how we expressed displeasure because if we raised our voice even one iota, it stressed her out and made her pee again.

Those days were difficult. Even when she knew we were taking her out for potty she'd get excited, and it just came out before we could actually get her through the door. We gave a stern *no* when she slipped up, immediately took her out and if she peed again outdoors, she got a reward. I hated giving her that potty treat if she'd peed in the house first. It felt like I was rewarding her for bad behavior, but I was following the advice from the dog experts, which for us came from several sources.

We immersed ourselves in reading books and articles with an emphasis on retraining a problem dog, and discovered that the advice of one trainer often contradicted another. We watched several dog training shows on TV, the most helpful being Victoria Stilwell's *It's Me or the Dog*. We sought advice in dog training forums, and from everyone we knew with a well-trained dog. We didn't choose the recommended path of hiring a dog trainer to help us, but trusted that our perseverance would eventually override Dakota's stubborn refusal to give up the bad habits. It was not an easy road.

The hardest times were in the evenings when we came home from work. Dakota had held it all day and she was fully loaded. We kept the dog crate next to the door in the hopes of getting her out of the house before she let loose. In the beginning it didn't work. The minute her feet cleared the door to the crate the pee was coming out. We continued as fast as we could out to the back yard with Dakota peeing all the way down the outside stairs. We took her directly to the pee pee spot where she peed even more. Dakota's bladder seemed to be an eternal spring which never stopped flowing.

Mornings were dicey as well. She'd held it all night long and thus woke up fully loaded. I never delayed in taking her out in the morning. I'd throw on a bathrobe and get her out the door as quickly as possible, not delaying even for my own morning potty.

There were times when it felt hopeless. We thought we'd never get her to stop peeing indoors. Ten weeks after adopting Dakota — putting her at almost ten months old — we finally had a breakthrough. For the first time ever I did not take Dakota out immediately after getting up in the morning. I pottied myself first and got fully dressed before taking her out, and still she held it. That showed incredible progress for her.

After ten weeks of diligent potty training she was not only holding it all night, Dakota had progressed from peeing many times a day in the house to only once or twice a month. We no longer had to keep the carpet shampooer out in the middle of the room ready to fire up. We were able to stash it back in the closet where it belonged — hidden and out of the way. Dakota had truly made incredible progress.

We learned several tricks of the trade in dealing with Dakota's potty problem. It wasn't enough to simply reward her for pottying outdoors. We needed to anticipate what caused her to pee in the house and nip it in the bud — staying one step ahead of her at all times. We needed to teach her new habits to replace the old, bad habits. Most of all we had to have patience. That was the hardest part.

Tricks of the trade
(Techniques for potty training)

During the night

It's normal for me to get up several times during the night, so when I got up for my own needs I'd throw on a bathrobe and take Dakota out. Even during those horrible first weeks Dakota never once peed in the bedroom at night. That in itself was amazing. Still, I took her out not wanting to push my luck. Hauling out the carpet shampooer in the dead of night did not appeal to me.

Once I saw that she seemed willing to hold it at night, I cut back from three times a night to two times, then down to one time, then finally not at all. However, the moment I woke up in the morning, I'd rush her down the stairs and out the door. I didn't dare make her wait, even for me to go pee. I figured if she'd been good enough to hold it all night, I wasn't about to tempt the fates.

You're with me

In the early days I kept Dakota with me at all times in the house. I literally made her follow me around the house as I went about my day. If I was going upstairs, I'd hook my finger under her collar and guide her up the stairs with me saying, *you're with me*. This became our daily routine. The goal was to keep her under my supervision at all times so that if she showed any signs of potty in the house (or any other bad behavior) I could immediately nip it in the bud.

This was pretty effective overall in her training. It also produced an unexpected result. She learned the command *you're with me* simply by repetition. I wasn't trying to teach her the words— I just simply said them anytime I made her stay with me and eventually, anytime I left the room or said those words, she would immediately follow. It became her habit to follow me around the house. She also learned my very predictable routine and knew that on certain days she was going to spend the day upstairs with me as I worked at the computer. She eventually graduated to having freedom of whatever floor I was on without needing constant supervision. On those days she would snooze in the bedroom.

Location, location

We kept the dog crate next to the back door to minimize the time it took to get her out the door after she'd held it while we were gone. This was an important step. Once she was able to hold it until she got all the way out to the potty spot, we moved the crate farther from the door. If she slipped up, the crate went back to the original location for a week or so. Forwards and backwards, that's how we progressed.

Potty treats

We rewarded Dakota with potty treats when she peed outdoors. We went through so many potty treats that we didn't use fancy schmancy expensive treats — we used one single piece of dog food. Her normal food came in small pieces and the potty treats were much bigger and a different flavor. For Dakota, that one nugget was enough to excite her and we kept a bowl of potty treats near the back door.

It didn't take long for Dakota to expect a potty treat for peeing outdoors. Once she got the hang of it and peed outdoors on command, I started delaying the treat until she was back in the house. This paved the way for other types of training later on.

After we fenced in the back yard, I was able to let her out unsupervised and reward her for coming back after pottying. In other words, the potty treat eventually became a reward for coming back, rather than a reward for pottying outdoors. Once indoors she'd sit next to the door and wait for the treat. I'd say *catch* and toss it to her. She learned to catch the potty treat in midair and she learned a new word — *catch*.

Several weeks later when Dakota started losing interest in the nuggets of dog food, we switched to raw baby carrots. Initially she was hesitant over this new edible, but once she'd eaten a couple, she fully embraced the carrots and they became a desirable treat for her.

Dog owners often overlook potential treats that don't fit the standard concept of a hunk of meat or a piece of cheese. There are a number of raw vegetables that your dog might embrace if you give it half a chance. Raw carrots, cabbage hearts, and broccoli stems are some of the treats we give our dogs.

Be aware that there are foods you should never give your dog: garlic, onions, chocolate, macadamia nuts, avocados, grapes, and raisins. They can make your dog very sick or even kill your dog. Contrary to popular belief, raw meat and eggs can harm your dog as well. Dogs are just as susceptible to salmonella and e-coli as we are, according to an article on the ASPCA website entitled, *Raw Food Diets May Be Dangerous For Pets*. Moldy foods should also be avoided. If it isn't fresh enough for you to eat, you shouldn't be giving it to your dog.

Water restrictions

In the beginning, we restricted Dakota's water intake. I searched the internet high and low for specific recommendations on how much water we should be giving her. While it was easy to find information on how much food she should get, I couldn't find a single reference as to how much water she should drink in a day, and this was an important factor in potty training.

One of the dog training shows on television had an episode about dogs peeing in the house, and the featured dog was a tiny little dog. The owners made sure that the dog had a full bowl of water at all times and this was causing him to pee in the house.

The dog trainer held up a small glass and said, "This is the size of your dog's bladder…" and then lined up how many glasses of water the dog actually drank in a day, "…and this is how much water you are giving your dog all at once. How can you expect him to hold all these glasses of water with his tiny little bladder?"

Dakota's water bowl held two 8-ounce glasses of water. I had no idea how big her bladder was, but I knew that she weighed about 60 pounds. I weigh more than twice that and I should consume six to eight 8-ounce glasses of water per day, so by those calculations the most Dakota should be getting was three or four 8-ounce glasses full per day.

Attempting to compare her needs to my own was prone to error as I was using the six to eight glasses for humans calculation based on what I'd always been told. In addition, this offered no differentiation between a human who weighed 100 pounds versus a human who weighed 250 pounds, but it was the best I had to work with.

I started out giving her 8 ounces first thing in the morning, and taking her out to pee several times before I left for work. The rest of her water quota was given as soon as I got home, but removed after dinner. I didn't give her any after dinner because I wanted to make sure that she was empty before bedtime. Planning for long stretches of hours when you won't be taking them outside for potty is important, as long as you compensate by giving more water at a different time that day.

As Dakota learned to hold her pee, I increased her morning quota. If I increased it too much and she peed on the carpet, then the next day I'd go to a smaller morning quantity again. This was trial and error. If I gave her *this much* she would pee — if I gave her *that much* she wouldn't pee.

Eventually I was able to stop measuring and just fill her water bowl when it was empty — even before leaving her on a workday, and even just before bedtime.

Today you can actually find specific water recommendations for dogs on the internet, and they are sophisticated enough to account for body weight, age, and several other factors.

Go directly to jail — do not pass go

If Dakota peed out of excitement or stress, we did not punish her. We made it very clear that we were displeased but we did not put any consequences onto it. However, if she peed out of spite, we did punish her. We took her outside to let her finish the job and then we put her in the dog crate for a little while. We thought of it as jail time for bad behavior.

The issue of using a crate for time-out is controversial because successful crate training hinges on your dog accepting the crate as his happy den. Punishment time-out will not make for happy crate time, and it's better to use a small room such as a bathroom. Dakota was still in a destructive phase, so we couldn't leave her alone even a bathroom which limited our options.

The ASPCA has an article on its website entitled, *Using Time-Outs Effectively*, and it covers when you should and shouldn't use time-outs, as well as how to use them effectively. Dakota's scenario isn't covered specifically, but as even the issue of spite pee is controversial, it's probably not a recommended use.

DAKOTA WITH A COCKY ATTITUDE

Those first months were so bad and her pee problem was so severe that we simply tried every method we could think of to break this horrible habit of hers — and that's exactly what it is, a very bad habit.

How can you tell what kind of pee it is? How can you tell the difference between a stress pee, an excited pee, and a spiteful pee? Consider the circumstances that led up to it. If you're playing ball with your dog in the house and he squats and pees, then this is an excited pee. If you walk in the door after being gone for many hours and he pees then this, too, is an excited pee. If he did something wrong and you've just chastised him it might be a stress pee or it might be a spiteful pee, and punishing a stress pee will just lead to more stress.

We learned to read Dakota's body language to determine whether she was stressed, happy, or mad at us. This is important if you'll be using different strategies depending on your dog's reason for the wrongdoing.

If Dakota was stressed, her eyes looked worried and she was breathing hard. If she was cocky or mad her demeanor was full of attitude, bad attitude, and it showed. The spiteful pees almost always occurred if she'd been bullying Gypsy Rose and got in trouble for it.

Rubbing her nose in it

This is yesterday's news — the old school method of potty training, and it is no longer recommended for teaching a dog not to potty in the house. Yes, your grandparents probably did it, because that's what the dog trainers of the 1800s and early 1900s told them to do.

The 1921 book, *All About Dogs* by Henri Vibert, gives us a glimpse at how rubbing a dog's nose in his business evolved. Vibert suggests that "rubbing his nose in it a couple of times will have a better effect than beating him up" and that you should never beat a pup for any reason. He was right.

Vibert wanted to break humans of beating their dogs, and rubbing their noses in poo was a gentler option. Trainers today are opting out of punishments altogether, in lieu of rewards.

Dog trainers view rubbing a dog's nose in the potty with the same sour puss that you'd see on a grumpy old man, or your grandfather's schoolmarm. And here's the thing, we successfully trained Dakota, with all of her issues, not to potty in the house *ever*, using positive training methods. If positive potty training can work on a dog like Dakota, it can work on your dog, too.

Today she is eight years old, and she's been solid for so many years that we can't even remember the last time she pottied in the house.

Paper training and pee pads

We did not attempt to paper train Dakota or teach her to potty on pee pads. This would have been counter-productive. The objective was to teach her to pee outside — not train her to pee inside. Paper training and pee pad training teach your dog to pee indoors. While this might be okay for a small dog who pees in tiny puddles, it would have been disastrous for a dog like Dakota who put out large quantities of urine, especially when we were trying to break her of the habit of peeing indoors.

Go pee pee

I used the phrase *go pee pee* every time she peed outdoors, and the phrase *go poopie* every time she pooped. She quickly learned the meaning of both phrases.

I also taught her the word *no* as an overall word of disapproval for whatever she was doing. The more words your dog knows, the better your relationship will be. Not only was I able to tell Dakota when I wanted her to go pee, I was able to communicate to her that potty in the house was bad.

You need to be able to communicate with your dog to tell them what you want, otherwise they won't know. Dogs aren't mind readers. The added benefit of knowing the difference between the two types of potty allowed us greater control of our dogs' potty habits when we took them on road trips.

Don't get her over-excited in the house

To cut down on the excited potty accidents, we did not play with Dakota in the house. We did not throw the ball, wrestle with her, or play tug of war. We did not do anything in the house to get her all revved up and excited. The goal was to remove the reasons she did it in the house in order to give us time to create better potty habits in her. This was one of the most difficult rules we had to follow. Dakota was young and full of energy and she needed to play. It was hard not to play with her indoors, but there was just no way around it — at least not in the beginning.

All we could do for Dakota in the house was to calmly pet her or give her chew toys to keep her busy, much like giving a baby a pacifier. Dakota went through a lot of chewies in those first months with us. We gave her hard bones, rawhide bones, and cow hooves to chew on. The dog experts are against all of these chewies with good reason, but for Dakota's early days with us, it was a risk that we chose to take. The dangers of giving your dog chewies is the subject of a later chapter.

Empty the dog

As Dakota's potty accidents became less and less frequent, we gradually began playing with her briefly indoors. It was critical to take her out for potty before attempting to play with her in the house. We called this *Emptying the Dog*. If we forgot, it was a guarantee that she'd let loose on the carpeting during play. Dakota was never truly empty but it helped. I'd never seen a dog that could pee as much as Dakota — she stayed fully loaded. She peed so much that we had her tested for kidney and bladder problems, but she was in perfect health.

The concept was simple: We'd empty the dog, play with her in the house for a few brief moments, and then take her outside for potty before she got to the pee point. There was a lot of guesswork involved as to when that point would come, and we often relied on her body language.

Sometimes Dakota would stop in mid-play to sniff the floor as if she thought she'd had an accident and was checking. Sometimes it was in the way she held her back-end as if she were clenching. The signs were often subtle and we could never be certain, but if we were in the least bit concerned, out she'd go for a potty break.

The back door became a revolving door — in and out and in and out as we tried to keep her as empty as possible. I worried that we were taking her out too often and that she was playing us to get a potty treat.

By the time she was two years old she did achieve the golden goal of being able to play rambunctiously in the house without letting loose. This was a long time coming but she did finally get there and today, we don't need to restrict her indoor play.

Who dictates potty time?

Dakota adopted the habit of sitting or laying by the back door when she wanted to go out. Initially we honored such requests but this was a sticky point. On the one hand we wanted her to learn that potty outdoors was the only good potty; on the other hand I did not want to teach Dakota to be a bothersome Boss Dog who dictated her potty times to me. I wanted Dakota to learn that if she is indoors, she does not potty *ever*, and to hold it until we take her outdoors. I wanted her to learn that outdoors was on my timetable, not hers. Allowing your dog to dictate potty time is the same as allowing your dog to be Boss Dog. This is a dog who is allowed to rule the roost which opens up a whole slew of problems in itself.

Because of Dakota's severe potty issues we ended up compromising. In the evenings when we were watching television we did honor her requests to go out, but under no circumstances did I allow her to wake me up from sleeping. Oddly enough she never pestered me to go out when I was working from home. She seemed perfectly willing to hold it.

She held it all night during sleep hours, she held it if she was in the dog crate, and she held it when I was working at home until I took a break — so why was she so all-fired willing to let loose during the evening hours?

There wasn't a single square inch of carpeting that hadn't been peed on. The main difference in the evening hours was that Dakota went into excited play mode and she had access to our other dog Gypsy Rose. These two activities put her into high gear. She was also more likely to get into trouble and be chastised for doing something wrong in the evening. Learning your dog's triggers can help you to figure out how not to trip the trigger and eventually work toward teaching your dog not to react to the trigger at all.

Once we knew she could hold it, we stopped taking her out every time she asked which was several times in the course of a normal evening. It wasn't always about potty at that point, she just wanted go outside. I started telling her *we did that already* as a way of saying no, I'm not taking you out again, and she'd give up the vigil at the door.

How long does it take to potty train an adult dog? (Or... when can I put the mop away?)

Every article we read said that it can take up to six weeks to potty train an adult dog, as opposed to two weeks for a puppy. We did not find this true for Dakota. It took months to retrain her not to pee in the house. While she quickly learned to pee outdoors, and to pee on command outdoors, she still slipped up every time she was excited or stressed which was often during those first few months.

Dakota had to learn to trust us, to trust that this home wouldn't be yanked out from under her, and to trust that even if we were displeased with her it did not mean she'd be dragged off to the dog pound. Yo-yo dogs come with a lot of mental baggage and this affects their training curve. With every week that passed, her slip ups were less and less frequent. Dakota was improving.

Eight months after adopting her, Dakota was finally holding her pee even when highly excited but on occasion, if she was stressed, she'd still have an accident.

After ten months of diligently working with her to break the bad habits and establish new, good habits, Dakota had transformed from a dog who peed on the carpet several times a day, to only once or twice a month. She had progressed. She no longer peed in the house from excitement. The rare occasion when she did slip up was almost always because she was mad at us.

Still we made sure to empty the dog before we played with her in the house. This was one of our golden rules and it held us in good stead. Dakota was an incredibly happy dog and as time passed and she learned more good habits, our moments with her started to bring pleasure instead of constant work and frustration.

Our time with Dakota became a source of great happiness and joy and we were finally reaping the rewards of our hard work. Life was good.

.

Jockeying for Alpha Dog Position

Second order of business: Who's the boss?
(Who's the boss — you or the dog?)

In most households the dogs and owners would answer this question very differently, and it's one of the keys to successfully training your dog. Who dictates feeding time? Who dictates potty time? Who dictates when it's time to get up in the morning? Who dictates playtime? The Boss — that's who.

Dogs who wake you up from a sound sleep to take them out or feed them are Boss Dogs. Their owners have allowed them to dictate the rules and in the natural order of a dog pack, the Boss Dog doesn't have to obey anybody, ever. Even if a Boss Dog learns a command such as *sit*, *stay*, *come*, or *speak*, they will only obey the command if they want to. The Boss Dog is king of the castle and you are there for his amusement. You are there to do his bidding. Boss Dogs make the rules; they do not obey the rules of others.

Our next order of business was to establish ourselves as Boss Dog in the pecking order. There are very subtle things you can do to solidify your role as Leader of the Pack. Feeding time is the perfect place to start. You should dictate when feeding time is. Our schedules vary quite a bit through the week. We don't get up at the same time every day, so feeding time is sometime after we get up, which can be anywhere from 7 a.m. to 10 a.m. Contrary to what your dog would lead you to believe, a dog does not need to be fed at the exact same time every day any more than we do.

When feeding time does come, it's important that the dogs are *not* allowed underfoot while we're filling their food bowls. The dogs are banned from the area until given permission to enter. This is one of the easiest lessons to teach a dog.

Here's how it works: While you are filling the food and water bowls, the dog must stay just on the other side of the doorway. If he comes into the room before you've given him permission, then stop what you are doing and escort him back out — every time. Use the commands *sit* and *stay*. At first you'll be doing a lot of escorting, but dogs figure out very quickly that the food isn't going to become available until they stay put. This is a strong motivator.

Dogs respond to body language. It's the natural language of dogs. To teach Dakota to wait in the doorway, I started out by making her *sit* in the doorway with my body physically blocking her entry into the kitchen. Then with my hand up and palm out in the stop sign position I said *stay*, drawing the word out slowly and hypnotically. I faced her while doing this and slowly backed away so that I could maintain eye contact with her. If Dakota started to follow, I walked toward her — literally walking into her — to force her to back up until she was back in the doorway. Again I would tell her to *sit* and *stay*.

Be prepared for your dog to make a game of it. For the dog it's as simple as: "I run *into* the kitchen and they *shoo* me back out, then I *run back in* again. What great fun!" Be persistent, be firm, and eventually you will prevail.

Once your dog is sitting in the doorway, put the food and water bowls down. If he comes running before you give permission, immediately pick up the bowls and set them back on the counter. Escort the dog back out, tell him to *stay* and try again. Dakota had this one down in less than a week. She will now wait until she is given permission to enter.

The main reason dogs go to obedience training and then fail to obey even the simplest command is not because they don't understand, but because a Boss Dog doesn't have to obey anybody but himself in a dog pack. The Boss Dog, also known as the alpha dog, rules the roost so if you don't also establish yourself as alpha dog in addition to any obedience training, your dog may simply choose to ignore you because you aren't the boss — he is.

Your tone of voice
(This is not an option!)

I praised the dickens out of Dakota when she did good or obeyed a command, and when I gave a command it was stern but not angry. My tone of voice expected obedience. This is very important. You shouldn't be begging or wheedling for obedience. Your voice should never sound like you're saying *please*.

If Dakota was being stubborn I'd start a command with the phrase: *This is not an option.* I actually said those words to Dakota in the sternest voice I could muster if she wasn't obeying a command. I'd say *"This is not an option!"* and then I would repeat whatever command she was ignoring. At that point she usually obeyed. She realized I meant business. My saying those words out loud helped me to get into the right tone of voice. It helped me to reinforce myself mentally and get into the proper state of mind to expect obedience.

Dakota was a raw recruit. I thought of her as being in boot camp with me as Sarge. Every waking moment I had to be Sarge, the undisputed boss. Your tone of voice sends a strong message.

Talking to your dog in a high pitched voice sends a different type of message. If you want a quick way to propel your dog into excitement, talk rapidly in a high falsetto voice and watch how

47

quickly your dog revs up. We used high falsetto for rambunctious play once we could actually play with Dakota indoors, and we used it for praise. A low, almost growly tone sends a message of displeasure. Think in dog speak. Dogs growl as a way to send a message to one another. Your tone should reflect your message.

People were amazed at our other dog, Gypsy Rose. She knew over eighty different commands and phrases. You heard it right — more than eighty. Don't ever sell your dog short. They might surprise you with how much they can learn.

Dogs aren't as dumb as they want you to think
(If I play dumb, I'll get my way)

Many people mistake a dog's refusal to obey for being a dumb dog. I've heard people say, *"Oh, my dog is just dumb, he can't learn."* Such people don't realize that there is a big difference in a dog knowing what you want him to do, and actually doing it.

Dakota knew without a doubt what our bedtime routine was. She knew many of our routines. Some routines she honored quite happily but with others she played dumb — looking at me with a blank stare even when I knew that she knew exactly what was expected of her. She used the blank stare as a pretense. Dakota played dumb simply because she didn't want to obey. Dogs do that a lot and people often misunderstand it. Dog plays dumb and dog gets his way. SUCCESS! Boss Dog wins again!

Subtle reminders that you are Leader of the Pack
(Heads I win, tails you lose)

You must win at games. Dogs in the wild play games not only for fun but to establish — or challenge — leadership. If you are playing tug of war, in the end you better win with the toy in your hand. In all games you must win. You can give the toy back after you've won it, but you absolutely must win it. This strengthens your leadership role in the pack.

If your dog is laying in the doorway and you want through that doorway, the dog must move. In the natural order of things the lesser dogs move out of the way of the Boss Dogs. If you are stepping over or around your dog, you are sending the message that you are lesser in the pecking order. If he's in the way then move him out of the way and give the command *move*. Physically move him as you are saying *move*. You don't need to be rough about it but you do need to do it. If he's laying down, rouse him up and out of your way. He'll probably flop like a sack of potatoes in protest but if you are diligent, eventually he will get the message.

If he's on the sofa or in a chair where you want to sit, put him on the floor and say *move*. Before long all you'll need to do is say *move* and he will. It may feel rude and from a human perspective it is, but in the dog world it's simply the natural order of things. Boss Dogs are always given clear passage. Lesser dogs always move out of their way.

Feeding Time at the Zoo

The "not enough food" mentality
(Are you feeding your dog enough?)

In the early days, my husband was concerned that Dakota seemed hungry all the time — as if we weren't feeding her enough. I was feeding her exactly what the dog food package recommended for a dog her age and weight. They are not likely to recommend too little — they wouldn't make money that way. Dakota was gaining weight under our care and dogs don't gain weight if they're not getting enough food.

You cannot trust your dog to make decisions. Just because he's staring at you woefully with big, sad eyes, doesn't mean you should give him more food. I believe that Dakota's ferocious hunger was a byproduct of her old life of being underfed. I'd experienced this years earlier with a kitten I'd adopted.

Hadji came from a world of wild outdoor cats — homeless cats — and my friend Jessie fed them. Jessie collected scrap food from the restaurant she worked at and took the food scraps home in a big bucket. Once a day she would dump the bucket full of scrap food in a big mound on her front porch and all the wild cats would converge on it — no food bowls and no rules. The bigger, stronger, bullier cats ate. The smaller, weaker, wimpier cats got pushed away. Hadji was just a kitten so he got pushed away a lot.

Hadji came into my home with the *not enough food* mentality and he was overly focused on food for a very long time. He never felt satisfied that he was getting enough. He panicked when he saw our other cat eating as if afraid she would eat his portion. He was afraid of going without. He was afraid of being left hungry.

Eventually, once he realized that twice a day he got fed like clockwork and that he wouldn't have to fight for food, he settled down and relaxed. Hadji stopped being afraid of going hungry. He became comfortable enough that he'd actually leave food in his bowl, picking at it all day without a care in the world.

Dakota reminded me of Hadji. She came to us with her ribcage jutting out so it was a good bet that she came to us with the same fear of going hungry. Her actions mirrored Hadji's exactly. My philosophy was to feed her as directed and demonstrate to her that I would protect her food from other dogs. I trusted that eventually she would stop acting as if she were starving. Some dogs will overeat if left to their own portions and I believe that Dakota was one of them.

Obviously if your dog acts as if he's starving and you know he's not, then you need to have your veterinarian check for worms or other health problems. Dakota did turn out to have worms that she'd caught when we boarded her for a week. I hate boarding for that reason.

Begging at the Table

Begging at the table and pestering for attention (More Boss Dog tactics)

Boss Dog strikes again. There is nothing innocent in the dog world. Almost every action boils down to posturing for position as alpha dog. Remember the rule about feeding time where you dictate the terms? Rewarding your dog for begging sends a very clear message: *Dog is boss — dog demands food — you will comply.* You have been assimilated. You are now his butler.

The same holds true with pestering for attention. If your dog is rewarded every time he pesters for attention, then he is getting a strong message from you: the dog makes the rules and dictates the terms. He wants attention and if you give it, he rises up the ladder to Bosshood. You have to say *no* and mean it.

While we are eating the dogs are not allowed to bother us. They must stay at a distance and not make eye contact with us or stare at our food. In teaching this, you may need to get up several times and escort the dog to a safe distance while issuing the *stay* command. If you are persistent, it will work. The key to all dog training is persistence and leadership. Establish a rule and enforce it — every time — not just sometimes here and there, but *every time*.

Your guests must also follow the rules that you set down for your dog. If you don't slip your dog food while you're eating then neither should your guests, regardless of how they treat their own dogs at home. In addition, if someone brings a dog to your home, you should be careful not to treat the dogs differently in front of each other.

This can be a very sticky point if your guests treat their dogs differently than you treat yours. We often have guests for Thanksgiving week and they usually bring their dog, who is accustomed to being fed from the dinner table — a custom that is taboo in our home. We had to set down a very strict rule for Thanksgiving dinner that all dogs got put away while we ate, in order to be fair to the dogs.

Dakota was shuffled off to the bedroom while their dog was put in a crate during the meal. This was not the normal situation for either dog, but it was the only way to enforce our rule of not feeding dogs from the dinner table. It was the only way to ensure that Dakota did not watch another dog being fed from the table, which would also have sent the message to Dakota that the other dog was boss over her. This was a message we didn't want to send. There's a lot at stake with the choices you make and it's up to you as Boss Dog to establish fair rules for all of the dogs in your pack.

Multi-Dog Household

Did they say good with other dogs?
(Gypsy Rose was not amused)

Our theory that a doggie friend would be great fun for Gypsy Rose was shot down pretty quickly. Once Gypsy Rose realized that Dakota was butting into her domain permanently, she was not amused.

Gypsy Rose had been an only dog for over ten years. The concept of sharing her attention, her space, her toys and chewies — this did not make her happy. Dakota didn't help. Dakota went out of her way to butt in front of Gypsy Rose for attention, for food, for everything. She tormented Gypsy Rose mercilessly. Dakota was a bratty teenager and Gypsy Rose was an old fogey. It was not the best mix. So much for Dakota being "good with other dogs" as we'd been told — so much for our assumption that Gypsy Rose would enjoy having another dog to play with.

To make matters worse, Gypsy Rose, who had literally been the perfect dog, started misbehaving. Dakota needed a LOT of attention to retrain and Gypsy Rose didn't appreciate this young upstart taking over her revered place in the household. Instead of Gypsy Rose being a good influence on Dakota, the exact opposite happened. Another assumption was shot down.

In addition we felt guilty. Gypsy Rose, who should have been basking in glory in her golden years, was instead wallowing in misery. Look what we'd done to her, our perfect dog who did not deserve this.

It's harder with two dogs
(Who are you talking to?)

It's harder with two dogs. While I was working to teach Dakota a new command, Gypsy Rose was obeying every command I gave Dakota. That was distracting for Dakota. It was a challenge to keep Dakota's attention focused on me. She was too busy watching Gypsy Rose dancing around trying to please me. To avoid this, it's better to work with the dogs separately.

With two dogs we had some serious jealously problems. Gypsy Rose had another dog butting into her territory and Dakota just wanted it all for herself. The end result was that both dogs were extremely jealous of the other. Gypsy Rose simply went off to sulk when Dakota browbeat her. Dakota's indoor tactics relied heavily on a get-in-your-face strategy and if she'd been a human, the forefinger would have been jabbing Gypsy Rose in the shoulder. No physical injury occurred but the mental harassment was just as effective.

Dakota was such a bully that Gypsy Rose would go off and cower in a corner. She didn't want to even walk past Dakota. Gypsy Rose was so miserable that she started to get snotty with us and we couldn't blame her. We'd brought a domineering dog into our home who was notorious for bully tactics and nipping, though she didn't ever break skin.

For Dakota, nipping was the natural order of things. She's part Australian Cattle Dog. That means she was bred to move in fast, nip at the heels of the cattle to herd them in a particular direction, and then quickly dart away to avoid getting kicked. This was in her nature and it produced challenges of its own for both us and Gypsy Rose. Know what your dog was bred to do and be prepared for how it will impact your dog's behavior.

It was hard having two dogs that were so mismatched — really hard. I didn't expect this level of difficulty. Gypsy Rose taunted Dakota, egging her on to mischief, which interfered with our training. Dakota was young and full of spit and energy. She wanted to do things that we didn't want her to do, and Gypsy Rose took full advantage of that. Dakota would actually have been doing pretty well except that with Gypsy Rose egging her on, she simply couldn't help but get into mischief.

Like a bad influence, our perfect dog did everything in her power to instigate Dakota to do all the things we were trying to break her of. I believe Gypsy Rose realized that she could get Dakota into trouble, and that's why she did it. Gypsy Rose did this during our *time-out* training attempts. If Dakota got in trouble, she got time-out either in the bathroom or her crate. Time-outs gave Gypsy Rose peace, and the chance to have us all to herself. Thus I stand by my theory — I believe that Gypsy Rose knew exactly what she was doing.

Dog squabbles
(I'll get you, my pretty)

Gypsy Rose was a peaceful, gentle dog. Dakota was a scrappy, street-smart problem child and she didn't want Gypsy Rose in her new territory. Dakota wanted to claim it all for herself — us included. She nipped at Gypsy Rose, shouldered her out of the way, blocked her path, and stared her down at every opportunity. Gypsy Rose made no attempt to counter-challenge.

Even when Dakota just wanted to play, we couldn't allow it. Dakota was a tough and tumble dog who liked to roughhouse, and Gypsy Rose was elderly — she was thirteen years old when we adopted Dakota. It was like having a teenage tomboy who wanted to wrestle with a grey haired old woman. We had waited too long to bring another dog into the house. Dakota's integration would have fared better had Gypsy Rose been several years younger. After Gypsy Rose passed away and we adopted another dog, it did indeed go more smoothly. The dogs were better matched in energy level, size, breed temperament, and age being only four years apart. In addition, Dakota was no longer the wayward menace, and the entire process was a breeze.

GYPSY ROSE AND DAKOTA FACE OFF

Many dog owners would just let the dogs battle it out for themselves but Gypsy Rose didn't deserve the crappy end of the stick, and dog challenges can easily become dog fights which end up in blood and stitches, so I intervened. I focused on teaching Dakota that it wasn't okay to nip at Gypsy Rose, jump on her, roughhouse with her, or push her away from the food bowls. My goal was to teach Dakota to respect Gypsy Rose by saying *no*, and by physically stopping her in order to demonstrate what I meant.

It took a long time for Dakota to embrace this concept and we had to resort to some radical training tactics. Dakota got more fun out of being bad than any deterrent could override. A word of caution however… if you attempt to get in between two dogs who are actually fighting, you could end up getting hurt.

The conflicts never escalated into a full blown blood war. My intervention was in establishing myself as Boss Dog rather than allowing Dakota to take the role, as was her goal. And as Boss Dog, I set down rules as to how the dogs were allowed to treat one another and interact.

It took eight months of intervention before they were getting along reasonably well. It took eight months of trying various tactics before I found one that worked. This was one of the hardest things for Dakota to learn — not because she couldn't learn it, but because she simply didn't want to and she was accustomed to getting her way — an expectation she'd acquired at her previous homes.

This is an important concept that many dog owners fail to grasp. Lack of early training, especially when it allows the dog free reign early on, leads to a dog like Dakota that ends up at the dog pound where they are usually euthanized. We were determined not to let that be Dakota's ultimate fate.

We went through months of trial and error before resorting to the big guns. We tried praise and reward. We tried a squirt bottle of water which was actually very effective except that Dakota figured out what distance it could squirt and she'd stay just beyond that distance. We searched high and low for a squirter which could shoot several feet but failed to find one even at the toy stores.

Attempting to actually catch hold of Dakota after a wrongdoing was a lost cause. God help you if you even tried.

Dakota could run like the wind and it didn't take long for her to figure out that she could run circles around the table and not get caught. They make cartoons out of some of the training methods we tried.

We devoured training articles on the internet from a variety of sources in addition to books and television programs on dog training. There was so much conflicting information.

Another failed effort was a rolled up newspaper. It wasn't to swat Dakota with, it was to smack the table to get her attention and startle her, as hitting wasn't part of our training program. Yet another tactic involved shaking a can full of pennies to get her attention. We tried time-out in the bathroom. We tried time-out in the crate. We literally went through months of trying different techniques to stop Dakota from tormenting Gypsy Rose. Within two weeks of pulling out the big guns, Dakota finally stopped the nonsense and the dogs became friends. They were finally able to play together. Dakota got the message that dog play had to be gentle. (More on the big guns later…)

A Word on Consistency

How long will it take for your dog to get the message?
(Or... when can I stop pulling my hair out?)

How long does it take for a dog to learn a new behavior? It depends on the dog, their age, and the behavior involved. It took less than three weeks for Dakota to learn to wait in the doorway while I put down her food. She had nothing to gain by doing it wrong. The food would not become available until she stayed in the doorway and waited for permission to enter.

Potty training took a lot longer as she had several issues relating to nervous peeing. Allegedly it takes two weeks to potty train a puppy and six weeks for an adult dog. For Dakota it took much longer than six weeks. While she did quickly learn to pee outside, she still had accidents indoors when she was excited, angry or stressed.

Our gauge for her progress was simple: How long between potty accidents? Was she showing improvement? The answer was yes, Dakota was definitely improving. She went from several accidents per day to just one or two, and then sometimes she'd go for a whole day without an accident, then two days, then three or more. We would put the carpet shampooer away believing that she was "fixed" only to haul it out again a few days later.

Sometimes we'd look at each other and ask, "*Can you remember the last time Dakota peed in the house?*" We could not remember. Then without warning, she'd let loose again once or twice before going for another long spell of being accident-free. It wasn't as simple as one day she had a problem, and the next day she was fixed.

If your dog is going for longer and longer periods between potty accidents or whatever behavior you're trying to stop, then he is improving and you are making progress. Let that be your gauge rather than a timetable.

A word on consistency
(How not to blow it)

Another issue is consistency and this is where many dog owners fail. They give a dog an old shoe to chew on and then not understand when he chews on their new shoes. You must be consistent. If you don't want your dog to chew on shoes, then *all* shoes should be off limits. Your dog's allowable toys should not be similar to forbidden items in your house.

Also, be careful not to send mixed messages. Dakota slept through the night without bothering us and Gypsy Rose, and without barking. It was one of the few good habits she came to us with. I wanted her to stay that way so I was very careful about what I did with her in the bedroom. I did not want to create a new bad behavior.

We did not pet her from bed because that would encourage her to bother us in bed and possibly wake us from a sound sleep. We did not play with her in the bedroom or allow dog toys in the bedroom even during the day. Our message was simple: The bedroom is for sleeping.

Training is in the small things that people don't think about. In those early days everything we did sent a message, and it was important to send the right message. Dakota needed to understand that when we were in bed she was not allowed to bother us, nudge us, bark at the moon, or jump around the room in play. Eventually — as in more than a year after she was solid with our bedtime routine — we were able to allow toys in the bedroom during the day. We were able to lighten up a little as long as she continued to follow our bedtime rules. Even then, however, we never kept toys available at night. As nighttime play was strictly forbidden, keeping toys around served no purpose except to tempt the fates. A slip up of any sort would put us back to enforcing the stricter set of rules.

Dogs will challenge you. Even after they've learned a new rule or routine, occasionally they will challenge the rule. Much like a toddler who discovers the joy of saying the word *no*, your dog will also challenge your authority from time to time, and this is normal.

There is no right or wrong set of household rules. Your rules should reflect your lifestyle. Everybody's lifestyle is different and dogs are adaptable. We don't allow dogs on the sofa. They are big dogs and they like to go outside and roll on smelly things like dead animals and duck poop. Trust me, if you ever see your dog outdoors rolling in ecstasy, you can bet that whatever he's rolling on would disgust you.

The rules you set forth in your home should make *you* happy. They don't need to be the same as the dog rules put forth by your family and friends with their own dogs. Just be consistent with whatever rules you set forth, and remember that if you do choose to allow your dog on the couch, as Boss Dog you are allowed your choice of where to sit. If the dog is in your way, he must move so that you can maintain your alpha dog status.

Let me entertain you
(I'll make you laugh and forget about your stinky rules)

Sometimes it's hard to be consistent. One of our jobs was to teach Dakota which items she could chew on. The rule was simple: These are your legal chew toys, and everything else is forbidden. If we didn't give it to you, then don't touch it.

Most things in the house were new to her and she didn't have a clue as to what was legal. We were pretty certain she hadn't spent much time in a house prior to our adopting her. Even the concept of a window was something that she didn't initially understand. She did not realize that she could watch the world through a window until she'd been with us for a while. Outdoors she easily recognized the objects of nature, but indoors everything was strange and alien to her.

Dakota was inquisitive and wanted to explore this fascinating new world we'd brought her into. One night we were watching television and Dakota came trotting into the living room carrying an empty one gallon milk jug that had been sitting on the floor next to the garbage can in the kitchen. We busted out laughing at the sight of Dakota proudly toting that yellow milk jug which was bigger than her head. She carried it by the handle, and it flopped around as she walked. Dakota was so innocent. She had no idea that the milk jug was illegal. It was hard to spoil not only her joy but our own as well. We had to stifle the laughter as best we could, muster up a stern tone, and take the milk jug away with a firm *no*.

The cutest things are often illegal so people let the cuteness win. Dogs end up at the dog pound because owners laugh instead of correcting amusing mistakes. What's cute for a little puppy — such as jumping up on your leg — becomes irritating and even dangerous when the puppy grows into a great big dog. Letting your small puppy pull you along on a leash to chase after a bug starts out cute, but soon becomes impossible when he grows up to weigh 120 pounds of solid muscle and wants to chase after bigger game with you hanging on for dear life.

No matter how cute the dirty deed is, you absolutely must nip it in the bud and keep on nipping it until that bud gives up. Dakota tried again on other nights and we steadfastly stifled the laughter and sent a firm *no* message. She doesn't bother milk jugs now. Dakota has found other, legal ways to be cute and make us laugh. Your dog doesn't need to get into trouble to amuse you. Trust me on this.

If at First You Don't Succeed, Pull Out the Big Guns

If one training method fails, try another (Resorting to stronger tactics)

One thing you'll discover if you talk to different dog trainers is that there are as many ways to train a dog as there are experts. Watch the dog training shows on television. I know of several in our neck of the woods and each has a different focus.

Read dog training books. Take an obedience class with your dog. Learn how to be a good teacher, and be flexible with your training method. If a particular technique isn't working for your dog, be prepared to try a different tactic if you've truly given the first technique every chance to succeed.

For example, a common method for training a dog not to pull when you're walking him on a leash is to immediately do an about-face and walk in the opposite direction. This works well with young dogs and small dogs. However, if you're trying to walk a big, strong dog that wasn't properly leash-trained as a puppy, you might find yourself in a dangerous tug-of-war.

A strong dog can pull you down and injure you with their eagerness to get somewhere. People have actually fallen down and broken bones in failed attempts to hold on to a strong dog. In such cases you may need to resort to special collars or harnesses when the preferred training method fails.

There are several types of walking collars and harnesses to help you control a strong, willful dog. Some of them lift the dog off the ground if they try to pull, while others turn the dog's head to the side. Both are recommended over choke collars and prong collars which can injure a dog's trachea, but I'd be afraid of breaking my dog's neck with the head-turning collar. I don't know what the statistics are for effectiveness, or for the safety of your dog. Another type of harness has the leash ring at the dog's chest so if he tries to pull, it turns him around toward you at the chest. They even make whistle-harnesses that blow a whistle when the dog pulls. The bottom line is that it's far better to leash-train your dog as a pup to avoid the problem in the first place, than to later resort to devices that might injure your dog, and which may not work for you anyways.

We did not resort to special harnesses or collars for walking Dakota, but we did resort to a special collar to control Dakota in our fenced back yard. Believe it or not, she did create challenges even then.

Dakota was a problem child. The first thing she did on a nylon leash was to grab the leash in her teeth and chew it in half so quickly that I didn't realize what she was doing until it was too late. Before we installed a fence, I'd taken her out to potty in the back yard and as a treat afterward, I allowed her to sniff the world at her leisure. When Dakota found something of interest, her nose glued to the ground and stayed there for what seemed like an eternity. Instead of watching her, I looked off in another direction. Big mistake.

While my eyes were fixated over yonder, her teeth fixated on the leash and when I turned back toward her, the leash was chewed 90% of the way through. Thirty seconds more and she'd have been off and running. We gave up the nylon leash for a chain leash. Lesson learned: Never take your eye off the dog when leash-walking.

She did the same thing when we attempted to tie her out on a 50 foot long rope. We were looking for a way to allow Dakota to spend time outdoors with us. Dakota chewed through the rope in a millisecond and was off and running up the street. She was so quick to do this that I figured she'd learned it long before we ever adopted her.

We weren't trying to tie her out by herself — this was supposed to be a family gathering in the back yard with Dakota having more freedom than a leash offered. We made one attempt to put her on a chain attached to a 20 foot overhead run, but she ran hither and yon like a madman, reached the end running at full speed, did a flip in midair and landed hard. We were afraid she'd break a leg so we nixed that plan as well. We had no way of allowing Dakota a semblance of freedom in the back yard.

She needed a way to run and exercise, so we installed a six foot privacy fence, but even this did not work out as perfectly as we'd hoped. The minute Dakota tasted freedom off-leash, she absolutely refused to obey commands. Dog trainers recommend using a 30 foot leash to train a dog outdoors so that they can't just blow you off, and this is great when working with a puppy, but Dakota's pre-existing habit of chewing through a leash nixed that plan, and a 30 foot chain is hard to handle. In addition, she found a way past the six foot fence and was off and running. Dakota didn't make anything easy.

If we were working in the garden or just hanging out in the back yard for fun, we wanted both dogs to join us. Dakota made that impossible. She took full advantage of our inability to catch her and tormented Gypsy Rose. Dakota jumped on and body slammed her, and there was nothing we could do to stop it.

Dakota was a strong dog and the one time she body slammed my husband Bear, he ended up with a six-inch round, livid purple bruise. When she did it to me, it hurt so much that I thought I'd broken a bone and I sat on the ground for a long time. Dakota was just a rough-and-tumble dog by her very nature, on top of never having been trained to curb that nature, and Gypsy Rose was just too old for the onslaught.

Dakota also chased Gypsy Rose around the yard nipping at her heels, and Gypsy Rose was clearly not amused. These weren't dog games that our elderly dog embraced. When Gypsy Rose passed away and we later adopted a dog whose youth and breed better matched Dakota's, the two dogs joyfully played chase-me games, and they became best friends. But it wasn't an option for Gypsy Rose and Dakota, too ill-suited to one another. Short of bringing only one dog out at a time, we had no means of addressing this wrinkle in the grand plan and it frustrated the hell out of us that our fence investment seemed all for naught.

We needed big guns — very big guns. As a last ditch effort, we invested in a buzz collar for outdoor training. This flies in the face of positive-reinforcement training and it's one of those issues that polarizes debates over dog training techniques. Dakota absolutely needed freedom to take advantage of our back yard for exercise, which is nearly three-quarters of an acre. She needed to run, and explore the woods, and roll in the grass, and just *be*. We needed a safe way to allow both dogs out at the same time for family outings.

Buzz collars emit an electric shock via remote control, along the same lines as an invisible fence. We chose a collar that had options for sound only, and graduating zap levels. This was a godsend. After just a couple of zaps Dakota got the message that obedience wasn't just for when we're in a 10x10 room or when she was on a leash; obedience was expected *everywhere*.

The buzz collar allowed us to protect Gypsy Rose physically and preserve her peace in those final two years of her life. The first time we hit the zapper, Dakota was caught completely off guard. We'd given her every warning, including triggering the sound button first so that she learned that if she heard the beep, and still blew us off, a zap might follow. Being an anomaly, she tested the waters, harassing Gypsy Rose again.

We knew how painful her antics could be so when she jumped on, body slammed, or nipped at Gypsy Rose, I'd give a verbal *no*, followed by a beep, and if she continued, a zap. If all she did was run around Gypsy Rose without making physical contact, we let her be.

It only took a couple of times before she realized that hey, the tables had turned and she was no longer free to be a holy terror. We were astounded. Dakota was so bull-headed and stubborn that we didn't think she'd respond, but the transformation was almost instantaneous, and after that she responded to just the warning beep.

Finally, we were able to let both dogs run loose in the fenced back yard. We had a reliable way of ensuring that Gypsy Rose didn't get injured as we had. Dakota got the message that she had to be gentle, and before long the two dogs were happily playing together. Gypsy Rose — for the first time since we adopted Dakota — enjoyed having a canine friend.

The lesson here is that when you adopt a puppy, as Dakota had been for her original owners, training is easy. If you let that puppy grow up without training, you end up with Dakota. I'm going to be blunt here — if you create the problem through lack of training, and then dump your dog off at the shelter as Dakota's owners did, then you've just sent your dog to his death.

Let me repeat — abandoning your dog to a shelter is *the same as* telling them it's okay to kill him, because that is exactly what will happen to a dog that you cannot handle. *Nobody* wants to adopt an adult, or semi-adult dog with behavioral problems. People who adopt dogs from shelters are looking for two types of dogs: puppies, and well-behaved dogs that just had a bad break. Your problem dog is as good as dead.

Dakota finding a forever home that was willing to take the time to work through her issues is the exception, the *very rare* exception. Had someone else adopted her that day, I believe absolutely that they'd have taken her back within the week to her final doom.

We resorted to punitive training techniques with Dakota such as the crate and the buzz collar, but neither were permanent. The buzz collar was only used to protect Gypsy Rose, not for general training, and once she passed away, the collar did not go back on Dakota again — ever — even after we adopted another dog.

Once Dakota could be left alone in the house without a crate, the crate was folded up and put away, and we worked diligently to take her to that point as quickly as we could achieve it. Granted it wasn't overnight, but the day did arrive, so time-out in the crate wasn't a lifelong event for her.

These were simply training tools to help us over the big hurdles. Most things she learned through praise, rewards, and persistence. Dakota made a lot of progress on those three things alone, and the dog we adopted later was young enough that we never needed to "resort" to anything — training Sierra was a breeze because we were her first trainers. We weren't fixing a problem that somebody else had created. In other words, if you are training a puppy, there shouldn't be any "resorting" to stronger tactics.

If you are in problem-solving mode as we were with Dakota, don't put a time table on your dog's progress. If he is improving, then your current training method is working even if it's working slowly. Only if you're not seeing any improvement whatsoever is it time to try a new training method.

When Praise Backfires

When praise backfires
(Bless her heart, she was really trying to please us)

In the retraining of Dakota, I did everything possible to create opportunities for praise, and to avoid situations that might set her up for failure.

I'd been working hard to break her habit of begging for food at the dinner table. One night we had a breakthrough. I was eating a thick, juicy steak, so I was a person of interest. She ignored me for awhile and then suddenly, the light bulb came on that I had desirable food.

She eyeballed me intently. I had a steak. It smelled really good and she wanted some. Dakota approached me and started pestering for food. I very sternly told her *go away*. I did not get up.

We'd spent many a night physically escorting her to a distance in our efforts to teach her the command *go away*, so she was getting the message but it wasn't fully hammered home yet. With a firm tone of voice I told her *go away*, and after a minute or so she went away and laid down.

Dakota had obeyed my command and I was very pleased, so I praised her. My happy voice rewarded her with a cheerful *good girl* which promptly backfired. She did not yet equate *good girl* with *stay put* and she immediately came to me for the petting reward which often followed a *good girl*. This of course was the exact opposite of what I wanted, so I had to tell her again to go away, and she did. For Dakota it was confusing. At that time *good girl* meant virtually the same to Dakota as *come here and we'll pet you*. The vicious cycle it caused for me to praise her was almost comical and I had to stop praising her so that she would finally settle down and stay put.

Lord of All Mealtimes
(Not so subtle reminder that I was leader of the pack)

We weren't the only ones that Dakota pestered for food. I had to play referee when feeding the dogs because Dakota's first instinct was to push Gypsy Rose away and eat her food first. Some folks will allow the dogs to work it out for themselves but I did not want Gypsy Rose to be bothered or go hungry, so I became Lord of All Mealtimes.

I physically stood between the two dogs and body blocked Dakota every time she attempted to bother Gypsy Rose. In other words, I put my body in between Dakota and Gypsy Rose's food bowl, and would not allow Dakota to go near it. I gave a stern *no* and physically propelled her back to her own food bowl, either by walking into her or leading her by the collar. Dakota didn't like it but she got the message. Before long I could intervene from a distance with a simple verbal warning and eventually, my intervention wasn't necessary at all.

I believed that part of Dakota's bullying for food stemmed from her history of not getting enough to eat. I don't know if her previous home had other dogs but the lady at the pet store had mentioned a sister, so perhaps Dakota had been forced to squabble for food at her old home. If her previous owners allowed the dogs to settle it amongst themselves and Dakota's sister was a bigger bully, it would explain why Dakota didn't get enough to eat. Her owners didn't care enough to ensure that she got a proper share of food — or perhaps they simply didn't feed her enough to begin with. Either way Dakota had a food fixation that needed to be addressed.

Once Gypsy Rose saw that I wasn't going to allow Dakota to bully her at mealtimes, she began to stand up for herself. Gypsy Rose would issue a warning when Dakota approached her bowl. My intervention taught a lesson to Gypsy Rose as well as Dakota. I was sending the very clear message that Gypsy Rose was was not lower on the totem pole than Dakota. Gypsy Rose started to understand this and stop cowering at Dakota's many bullying tactics. She even began to initiate playtime with Dakota although I had to oversee that as well since Dakota was prone to playing too roughly. With Dakota, nothing was ever simple.

Teaching Your Dog Words

Dogs aren't dumb
(So don't treat them like dummies)

One very important factor in Dakota's training was that for the most part I did not handle her in anger, but I was stern. I handled her like an old-fashioned schoolmarm who means business, and I fully expected Dakota to obey me. I did not hope that she would obey — I *expected* her to. I had high expectations and proceeded accordingly. I did not assume that she was too old or too dumb to be trained.

I knew that Dakota was intelligent and could learn anything that I wanted to teach her. I knew that she was capable of understanding many different words, phrases, and commands. I talked to Dakota as if she understood my every word, even when I said words she'd never heard before. I knew that with repetition, many of the words that were now gibberish would become clear.

For example, when it was time to go up to the deck after playing in the back yard, I said *up* as we went up the stairs. Initially Dakota didn't have a clue what I meant, but eventually she realized that going up the stairs and the word *up* were connected. I did this consistently both indoors and out — assigning a word or phrase to almost every action.

A dog who knows a lot of words will be not be as bored. They will be less likely to cause you problems. Dogs are highly intelligent and you need to give them things to think about besides how to get into trouble.

Because Gypsy Rose knew so many words, she listened every time we talked even if we weren't talking to her. Gypsy Rose listened for words that she understood and if she heard one her ears would perk up. She'd look to us to see if we were talking to her. Once she saw that nobody was paying attention to her she'd go back to her naptime.

Body Language

Reading your dog's body language
(How about learning a few dog words?)

Dogs have a lot to say if you learn to listen to them. A dog's body language speaks volumes of words — you just need to know how to interpret. I won't begin to go into the many variances of a dog's body language. Whole books have been written on the subject but there are a few things you can watch for.

Tail: Is his tail held high? Slumped down low between the legs? Wagging fast? Wagging slowly? Held stiffly straight out? When Dakota holds her tail high she's either happy, alert, or aggressive. When her tail gives a slow wag it usually means that Dakota is waiting for a cue, she's not sure what's going on and she is waiting to find out. A dog's tail is an excellent barometer of mood if you learn how to read it.

Hair on the back of the neck: Is the hair on the scruff of your dog's neck standing straight up? Dakota's does this when she's in aggressive mode toward Gypsy Rose or when someone comes to the front door.

Breathing: Soft and easy? Fast and hard? A dog's breathing actually changes in accordance with their emotional state. Rapid breathing or panting can indicate not only that he just ran a marathon or is hot, it can also indicate stress or the need to go potty.

Tongue, mouth and whiskers: Is the tongue hanging from the side of the mouth? Usually a dog in very happy play mode does this. Is the mouth closed, lips almost pursed, whiskers pushed forward? A dog's mouth can tell you a lot.

Stance: How is your dog standing? Is he standing still, alert, watching intently with his tail held stiffly out? Are his shoulders raised high, head held low? How far apart are the back feet? Close together and relaxed, or far apart in an attitude of readiness? Is he bowing with his front end on the ground and his rump in the air? Bowing usually indicates a request to play.

Ears on a pointy eared dog: Are they standing straight up? Facing forward? Sideways? Held flat against the head? Twitching? Dakota was notorious for twitching her ears when ignoring a command. It was her way of saying, "Ho hum." There are other reasons for twitchy ears such as bothersome bugs, but she was pretty consistent.

I'm not offering up interpretations for you. Just be aware that every part of a dog's body has a story to tell. If you pay attention, you'll see that your dog's body language is consistent. Start noticing how his body is when he's happy, angry, stressed, in trouble, alert, aggressive, passive, scared… and you'll begin to notice patterns.

How does your dog say No? (And when should you let him?)

Our dogs both sit down as their way of saying *no*. Sometimes it's a bad thing. They're saying, *"No, I'm not gonna and you can't make me!"* Sometimes it simply means, *"No, I don't need to go potty — we can go back inside."* Learning to interpret your dog's way of saying *no* will take you a long way in your dog training.

Once Dakota had peed outdoors, if I then tried to continue on to the poopie spot (which was anywhere in the wooded areas of the yard) sometimes she would grab the leash in her teeth as if to say STOP! She didn't need to poopie and was ready to go back in the house. She never once pooped in the house after sending this message so I assumed that I was reading her correctly.

Initially I hated to encourage the word *no* since I wasn't sure if she was being defiant or whether she simply didn't need to poop. Once Dakota grabbed the leash in her teeth to stop us from moving forward, she absolutely would not budge in any direction but toward the house. Once she saw that we were going in the desired direction she'd make a beeline for the back door, pulling hard on the leash, desperate to get back inside. I don't think she spent a lot of time indoors in her previous life and it was the only place she wanted to be.

Once I switched to a chain leash Dakota stopped grabbing the leash with her teeth and would instead sit down as her way of saying *no*. It was the same for Gypsy Rose. Sitting down on the way to the potty spot meant, *"No, I don't wanna go there"* or *"I don't need to go there."* Unlike potty training for pee pee, potty training for poopie went a lot faster.

At first Dakota pooped three times a day but as the months passed, it gradually went down to twice a day. Most adult dogs will only need to poop once a day if they're eating a good brand of dog food. The food you give them makes a big difference. Lower quality foods create more poop — there's less good stuff to digest and most of it comes out the other end.

We've used several brands including Science Diet, Bil-Jac, and Blue Buffalo, but there are many decent brands of dog food, and the quality can change even within a brand. What was high quality five years ago might not be today. Try an experiment. Buy a small bag of any cheap dog food and use it until the bag runs out. Monitor your dog's poop — how much and how often. Then go to a pet store and buy one of the choice brands that you won't find at the grocery store. Give it a couple of weeks and see if you notice a difference in the quantity or frequency of your dog's poop. If you notice a positive difference, then it's time to change brands. You can experiment with several brands this way.

Gypsy Rose in her early years had chronic diarrhea until we changed to a different brand of dog food. The vet said that she had some sort of food sensitivity. He switched her food and like magic, Gypsy Rose was fixed. Amazing! If your dog suffers from chronic diarrhea, *always* have him checked by your vet before assuming it's the dog food.

Eventually I learned to trust when Dakota indicated that she didn't need to poop, but the whole issue of allowing Dakota to say *no* was a sticky one. I had to balance my desire to fortify my alpha status versus some of her unique needs and panics from her previous experiences. I didn't want to push alpha if the issue wasn't alpha. Once she learned that she was safe with us, the bad memories from her old life would fade and so would the issues they produced such as her need to get back into the house as quickly as possible.

It took several months for Dakota to begin to trust in her new life. Eventually she stopped panicking to get back indoors as if somebody was going to yank her away and send her back to the dog pound. She began to enjoy being outdoors and she stopped being a stick-tight as she had been in the beginning — glued to my side in fear that I'd disappear the moment she looked away.

As for the issue of Dakota saying *no*, I had to differentiate between the acceptable *no* such as Dakota telling me that she didn't need to potty anymore, versus the defiant *no* that said, *"I'm not gonna and you can't make me!"* The defiant *no* required intervention. For example, Dakota didn't want to go to bed at night. As soon as she realized that we were headed for the bedroom, she'd hunker down in the hallway and refuse to go into the bedroom with us. She wasn't sleepy.

Dakota laid down in the hallway, a dog's favorite way of saying, *"No, I'm not gonna."* No amount of coaxing or pulling would budge her and I had to literally pick her up and carry-drag her into the bedroom. She was too big and heavy to fully lift up off the floor. Ideally you are supposed to encourage them do it on their own but if they've been allowed to be Boss Dog at some point in the past, it doesn't always work.

A good size strong dog cannot always be pulled along and a strong-willed dog cannot always be talked into things. Dakota was both strong and strong-willed. She had learned many tricks in her old life for getting her way. She had intelligence plus a mind of her own which made it harder to overcome her lack of previous training in some respects. Had we been training a puppy, we wouldn't have had this ongoing battle of wills because we would have established the pecking order from day one.

A dog who wants what you're peddling will learn faster. Dakota wanted to eat, so she quickly learned the food routine. She didn't want to go to bed at night, and even though she knew the bedtime routine, she didn't want to do it.

Dakota didn't appreciate being half-dragged into the bedroom with us every night. After a few nights of not letting her get her way, she stopped laying down in refusal although she did occasionally poke along slowly. Sometimes we had to get behind her and propel her along a bit but overall she got the message that bedtime was when we dictated — period. She was going to end up in the bedroom one way or another so she might as well come along on her own.

Once she gave up on defiance and followed our flow, she began to anticipate when it was time for bed and she would sometimes go up to the bedroom even before we did. Dogs are creatures of habit. Once she knew that she'd had her final potty of the day and any evening treats or playtime with us, it wasn't uncommon for her to head off to the bedroom. She knew that was the next thing we were supposed to do.

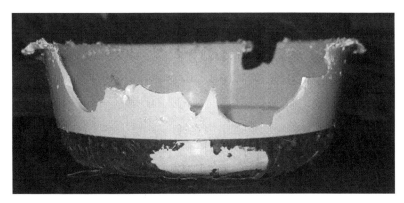

DAKOTA'S CHEWED UP FOOD BOWL

Dealing With Dog Chewing Problems

What had we gotten ourselves into?
(And how do we get out of it?)

How do you transform a dog who chews your world into pieces? Along with the many other problems we'd inherited with Dakota, she chewed things.

Three days after adopting her we had to go to work, which meant leaving her home alone for the day. We confined her to a portion of the garage with food, water, and dog toys. My husband got home first and nothing could have prepared him for what he walked into. Dakota had pooped everywhere. Not only had she pooped, she had managed to smear it all over herself, the floor, the dog food bowl, the water dispenser, and the dog toys we'd left for her, in spite of the fact that she had plenty of room to steer clear.

Subsequent days we came home to find that she'd chewed her dog bowls into teeny little pieces and had ripped open a bag of cement, scattering its contents hither and yon.

About a month after adopting Dakota, we invested in a dog crate and moved her into the house on our workdays. This solved some of her problems such as the barking all day, but she still chewed. We attempted to put a blanket in the crate but the very first day she chewed a two foot hole in it, so we took it out and she didn't get another one. We fed and watered her before we left and again when we got home. It wasn't intended as a permanent solution, only as a tool to help us through the transformation stage. The goal was for Dakota to have full run of the house as Gypsy Rose did, without restriction, and so everything we did was aimed to move her into that golden place of trust.

DAKOTA'S BLANKET WITH HOLES CHEWED IN IT

Several months later we went off on another vacation. It wasn't a dog vacation, so both dogs stayed home in the garage with a neighbor to look after them. We bought a 6x10 chain link dog kennel and put it in the garage for Dakota. We felt it best to keep them separate. We left Dakota with an automatic water dispenser, a heavy plastic dog food bowl, and we laid a thick carpet of hay down for her. We arranged for the girl next door to feed the dogs twice a day and take Gypsy Rose out as she'd done for us many times before. We did not have her take Dakota out walking, as we did not believe that she could handle Dakota's carpetbag of slick tricks. Dakota could smell an easy mark a mile away as far as what she could get away with.

Having seen the heartbreak that our friends experienced when their dogs got loose under the care of a dog sitter, we weren't about to give Dakota the key to Pandora's Box of Freedom. Our friends lost two dogs, both hit by a car after dashing out the door together. A third dog survived.

Why do dogs chew?
(Figure out the why and you're halfway to the solution)

The dog sitter reported that within 24 hours Dakota had destroyed the water dispenser. In spite of our efforts to make her comfortable, being in the garage stressed her and Dakota dealt with stress by chewing.

CHEWED UP BASE OF WATER DISPENSER

Dogs chew for a variety of reasons. A dog who is bored might be looking for a way to entertain themselves. Sometimes dog play gets a little rambunctious and objects get destroyed. Some dogs don't do well when left alone for too many hours. Some dogs even have issues if you ignore them a lot when you are at home.

Dogs need to be kept busy, especially active breeds like herding dogs and sporting dogs. If you don't provide them with outlets for their energy, they will make their own outlets. Young dogs of any breed are full of energy and if you don't exercise them, all of that pent up energy will find a way out — usually in a bad way. Dogs don't even start to calm down until they're about three years old.

Dakota was all of the above. She had abandonment fears so whenever we left her she became distressed. Being an Australian Cattle Dog/Siberian Husky mix put her in the high energy working dog category. In addition, Dakota was young and full of energy, and she was exuberant to have people who cared about her happiness and well-being.

Would you trust a toddler to his own devices? (Then why do you trust your dog?)

Dakota was a mouthy dog. She reminded us of a baby bird. Her mouth was always open with the expectation of latching onto something, and if it sensed an object nearby, it attempted to grab onto the object. It didn't even seem to be a conscious decision. Her mouth was a live thing unto itself. If something came into its range, she latched onto it and started to chew. It wasn't malicious — it just was.

In the early days we did not leave Dakota alone in the house out of sight. If she disappeared around a corner, I was hot on her tail. Dakota was in her curious stage, exploring the world around her like a young child discovering the wonders of the world for the first time.

Parents with young toddlers often child-proof their homes, making sure to cover electrical outlets, move glass objects off of low tables, install child-proof locks on low cupboards, use baby gates, put hook locks high up on screen doors, and so forth. The goal is to protect the child from injury, and to prevent your home from being destroyed by an innocent child who simply doesn't understand that knocking a glass vase off the table and breaking it is bad. It takes years to teach a child the many rules of life, and in the meantime you must watch over him.

Your dog is no different. Dogs don't know that chewing on electrical cords can kill them any more than toddlers do. Dogs aren't born into the world knowing that a table leg isn't an acceptable chew toy. Consider this: A dog in nature will chew on a tree branch and to your dog, the table leg is just another piece of wood. You must teach your dog just as you would a child: object by object. Don't leave your dog alone unsupervised with run of the house until you are confident that they can be trusted not to injure themselves or damage your home.

As Dakota explored this new world which was our home, we taught her, object by object, which items were taboo. At various times she grabbed an empty plastic milk jug, shoes, a wooden billy club, tin foil with meat drippings from the garbage can, berries off of potted plants (which is a dangerous habit if the berries happen to be poisonous), and a roll of toilet tissue sitting on the floor. We didn't catch her in time with the toilet tissue and she shredded it.

During those first months we never left her unsupervised in the house — ever. I made her follow me everywhere, hooking my finger under her collar and guiding her around the house with me as I moved from room to room.

If I was doing dishes, I made her stay in the kitchen with me. If we were in the living room watching television, she was expected to stay in the living room with us. When taking a shower, I took her into the bathroom with me and closed the door so that she couldn't leave. I blocked the stairway so that she had to stay on whatever floor I was on.

We didn't ever chastise her for attempting to leave the room — we simply prevented it. With the constant repetition, she got the message to stay close to us. Dogs learn by repetition and if you are consistent, they will get the message.

Bait and Switch
(I'll trade you this dog bone for that smelly old shoe)

DAKOTA CHEWING A GIGANTIC RAWHIDE BONE

I wanted to catch Dakota the minute she grabbed something so that I could tell her if it was legal or not. The goal was to teach her that unless it was something that we gave to her, she shouldn't touch it, and we were very careful in what we did give her.

This is where many people fail. If you play tug-of-war with an old sock, you are teaching your dog that socks are legal toys. If your dog has his own teddy bear, he may not realize that your children's teddy bears are taboo. If you tease him with a broom while sweeping, don't be surprised if your broom becomes his next chew toy. Your choices will impact your dog's behavior, so give thought to the items that you allow your dog to have.

If Dakota grabbed something illegal, I immediate took it away and made it clear that this object was forbidden, and then replaced it with something that she was allowed to have. In other words, you don't just take away the bad thing — this can cause a tantrum just as with a child. Instead, you trade it for something else. We went through a lot of dog chewies in that first year, more so than if we'd trained her from a pup.

We gave her hard bones, rawhide bones, and hooves to keep her teeth busy. There are dangers involved when using all of these chewies, but we had to divert her from chewing our house to pieces.

Dog treats can kill a dog (Even the ones you buy at the pet store)

Why are chewies dangerous? They can actually harm your dog. Small shards can break off of a hoof or bone, and if your dog swallows a piece with sharp points, it can pierce his stomach or intestinal lining and kill him. If your dog swallows a piece of rawhide or hoof that's too big, it can block the intestines and require surgery to remove, if it doesn't kill your dog first.

Even small pieces of rawhide can be dangerous. Rawhide swells up when wet, so what was a small piece going down becomes a much bigger piece once inside. Neither rawhide nor cow hooves break down quickly once ingested, so they can linger and build up with subsequent swallowings unless they simply pass through undigested.

A solid mass of any substance can cause an internal blockage that can be fatal to your dog. If you don't believe me, do a Google search. Type in "dangerous dog treats" or "dog treats kill" and you'll find page after page of scary news. And because deadly dog treats from China are the hot news topic of the day, you may need to search for "dangerous dog treats rawhides" or "dangerous dog treats hooves" specifically.

If Dakota hadn't been so difficult, if she'd not had so many needs and problems to solve, we wouldn't have given her so many of these dangerous treats. Safe treats don't offer much to a dog who needs to chew. We learned about the dangers the hard way, and thankfully Dakota survived her first brush with death.

One night she gave us quite a scare. It was related to swallowing the remnants of a hoof. Left to her own devices, Dakota would keep eating chewies until she'd ingested too much, so we had to monitor how much she was swallowing and take it away before she swallowed too much. Because of this, Dakota became paranoid.

She knew that sooner or later we'd take away her chewy so any unexpected movement on our part was suspect. She'd hurry up and try to eat as quickly as she could, sometimes swallowing big chunks in the process.

One night she'd gotten down to the last remnants of a cow hoof — a piece that we later discovered was about two inches in diameter. She saw me coming towards her and before I could snag the hoof, she swallowed it whole. I didn't know at the time how big a piece she had swallowed. It wasn't until it came out the other end that I had an inkling of the size. All I knew was that she'd swallowed a piece when she saw me coming, and I hoped it wasn't too big a piece.

Not long after, Dakota became ill. She tried to drink water but it immediately came back out as a projectile — Dakota was vomiting like a scene from *The Exorcist* movie. Initially it was as if the water never got fully down into her innards before it came up again, and I suspected that the chewy had created a blockage. She seemed to be breathing okay and her main distress appeared to be the inability to hold down water, so I did not take her to the vet, hoping that the object would work its way through.

It was a judgement call. I knew that the remnant did not have sharp edges to perforate as I'd seen it get whittled down over a period of days, so the issue revolved around it getting stuck. I stayed up with her all night, providing plenty of water and taking her out to the bathroom every time she asked. Dakota was agitated and pacing much of the night, but after the initial bout of bizarre vomiting, the water did start to settle and stay down.

After an exhausting night she passed the chunk of hoof. I poked sticks in her poop searching for the evidence and found a hard object which I assumed to be the culprit. Once she passed it, she was fine. Her distress was gone and the incident did not appear to have left permanent damage. Finally able to rest, we both slept most of that day.

Dogs die from swallowing objects that block their intestines, and surgical removal is often required. Blockages can escalate into complications such as cutting off the blood supply, which can cause gangrene in just a few hours. Like many dog owners, we did not realize how quickly this could have turned bad, and in sharing Dakota's story, I hope to educate others.

People can own dogs for their entire lives and never be aware of these dangers, because most dog training manuals or even obedience classes are geared toward basic training, not in-depth studies on alpha challenges and first aid. Most people learn dog ownership techniques from their parents, passed down from generation to generation, without ever giving thought to whether there is a better way.

After the big scare we watched Dakota like a hawk. If small pieces broke off her bones or hooves, we immediately took the pieces away and disposed of them. If her chewy got close to that dangerous size where swallowing it whole might cause a blockage, we tossed the chewy and gave her a new one. No matter what else we were doing, we kept one eye on Dakota with her chewy, monitoring for both how much she ingested and for big pieces. Losing Dakota just wasn't an option. In spite of all her problems we'd grown to love her dearly.

Rawhides weren't quite as bad but they didn't last long. Dakota could devour an average size rawhide bone in an hour, which was bad not only for her innards, but it didn't keep her teeth busy long enough. If Dakota was awake, she wanted to chew, and we finally hit on the solution. We bought the biggest rawhide bones we could find at $10 each. The big ones kept her busy for hours and she didn't actually swallow much.

In those early days, the giant rawhides were a godsend. While $10 seemed like a lot to spend on a single rawhide bone, they lasted for so long and kept her teeth so busy that they were well worth the price. Eventually, however, Dakota got the hang of how to peel them apart and within minutes would have a big chunk ready to swallow, so we stopped offering her the big rawhides, but by then she didn't need a pacifier any more.

In training to be the perfect dog
(Even when they're good, they're bad)

The time we put into potty training Dakota, dealing with the nervous pee issues, addressing the need to chew, and teaching her which items she could legally chew on, was time well invested. We had tackled her issues from many different angles, including teaching her words and playing fun games so that she wouldn't get bored and look for destructive outlets.

By the time Dakota was two years old we are able to leave her loose in the bedroom without incident (and without chewy toys of any kind) while we were at work. This was amazing progress for a dog who initially wanted to grab everything that came into her sphere and chew on it.

The chapter entitled "Training Your Dog to be Home Alone" details how we weaned Dakota from the crate. We were up to about three hours in the main part of the house, and the only incident we had was when we left a blanket on the floor. She chewed some pieces off of it. For some reason blankets on the floor defied our efforts to stop her chewing. Maybe it was a carryover from her old life. The only solution we found was to avoid leaving blankets on the floor — at least for several years.

We were also careful not to leave small, plastic objects on the floor. I had taken a box fan apart to clean it and forgot to put the feet back on. An hour later I found them chewed to pieces.

Your dog will not go from problem to perfect overnight. The fan feet incident happened months after we thought we could trust her but such incidents were rare, and they didn't happen at all if we were careful about what we left on the floor.

Dakota learned early on not to grab things off of tables so most of our efforts were spent on things lying on the floor. We trusted her enough to leave her for many hours in a room that we'd dog-proofed for the items that tempted her, once we weaned her from the crate. Remember, dog training is about creating new habits to replace the old ones and just as with a toddler, you may need to dog-proof your home while they are in the training stage.

Training Your Dog to Be Home Alone

Trust this wild-eyed bucking bronco home alone?
(You must be NUTS!)

If your goal is to free your dog from a crate when you are not at home, then read on. This is the next installment of Dakota's story. Believe it or not, we were successful in teaching Dakota to stay home alone with full run of the house on our workdays. This dog mastered the art of being home — unsupervised — without chewing or pottying in the house. It was nothing short of a miracle (and a lot of hard work retraining her).

Remember Dakota's wild beginnings with us when she smeared poop on everything in her reach, ripped open a bag of cement, and peed on almost every inch of our carpeting? She had chewed up plastic bowls, automatic water dispensers, coasters, rolls of toilet tissue, blankets, and a variety of small plastic objects. When left unsupervised Dakota was destructive, so on our workdays she was relegated to the crate. I don't know why they call it a crate — it looks like a cage to me.

In the beginning, we did not trust Dakota even in the crate. We were afraid that she would attempt to break out of jail, so we reinforced the crate with metal clips at all of the seams. In addition, we clipped the door latches. Dakota loose in the house would have been disastrous.

As it turns out our fears were not unfounded. I've read stories of dogs who did the very thing that we were afraid of — they forced their way out of a crate through the seams.

DOG CRATE AND REINFORCEMENT CLIPS

For us, however, the crate was a godsend. Dakota did not potty in the crate when we were at work. Neither did she bark. It wasn't our favorite option but we didn't have a better alternative. The crate we chose was much bigger than Dakota. She could stand up, sit up, turn around, lie down, and stretch out without being cramped. The crate allowed Dakota to be in the house when we were gone, and it was the first step in giving her freedom of the house.

Freedom must be earned
(Out of sight, out of my mind with worry)

Before we could undertake the next step, we had to make sure she was fully potty trained and that she wouldn't chew. You cannot expect a dog to be good when you are gone, if they aren't good when you are at home.

We did not attempt to wean Dakota from her crate until we were confident that she could, and would, hold her pee, and that we could reasonably trust her not to destroy things. This phase of training was gradual. Dakota had come to us godawful so it was going to take a lot for us to trust her with this very big step. This is another area where people fail. They leave their dog home alone without first having trained the dog not to chew or pee in the house, and then they don't understand when their house gets torn apart and pottied on.

In teaching Dakota not to be bad in the house, we kept her in our sight at all times so that we could immediately deal with potty and chewing issues. If she attempted to leave whatever room we were in, we'd call her back or follow her — *just as we would have with a toddler.*

Once she stopped grabbing things illegally while in our sight, she was ready to graduate to the next level. We'd let her disappear out of sight for a few minutes before following to check up on her. Baby steps — we took her training in baby steps. Once we knew she could be left alone for three or four minutes out of sight without incident, we'd let it go longer. Over the course of many months we began to trust her alone in other rooms, as long as she was on the same floor that we were on. We used a baby gate to block the stairway.

This is the first step in training a dog to be home alone with freedom in the house. First you must be able to trust them out of your sight when you are at home.

Home alone
(Will bad dog trash the house?)

Once you have achieved that goal, then you can start the next phase: leaving them alone in the house when you are outside. Initially this was also for just a few minutes — I left her loose in the house when I'd go out to get the mail or empty the garbage. A dog can get into mischief that quickly so again, we took this journey with her in stages.

The next step came when a neighbor stopped me to chit chat by the mailbox, which took Dakota to the next level of twenty minutes alone in the house. Dakota spent those minutes watching me. I could see her face in the window so I did not worry overmuch.

As the weeks passed I took every small opportunity to leave Dakota alone inside: when I took out the mail, talked to a neighbor in the driveway, mowed the lawn, trimmed the roses, or any activity that put me outside for a short period of time. When we reached that golden place where she could be left indoors while we were outdoors, we could then start weaning her from the crate when we were gone.

Moving on up
(Graduating from the crate)

She did not move from the crate to full run of the house in one step. The next goal we set out to achieve was to leave her alone in the bedroom with the door closed. She was already sleeping through the night loose in our bedroom without incident, so we began to put her in the bedroom with the door closed during the day when we were at home to get her used to the idea. We did this for very brief periods. Make sure to potty the dog first so that they are empty. It's better to prevent an accident than clean one up later. It's better for them to learn the right habit from the start than to break a bad habit later.

Again we took this in steps — five minutes, then ten, then twenty, and up to forty five minutes locked in the bedroom alone. Our bedroom was for sleeping. We never played with her in there so she associated this room with sleep or lying down quietly while waiting for us to get up in the morning. We removed several things from the bedroom that we thought might tempt her before moving to this phase of training: a phone sitting on the floor, a guitar, and shoes. We did not leave any temptations for her.

Moving into the penthouse
(Dakota earns a gold star)

Once she was accustomed to being locked in the bedroom, we started putting her in the bedroom instead of the crate if we were going out for a quick errand. When I say quick I mean *quick* — such as directly to the post office and back, or the bank and back — errands which only took a half hour start to finish. We did not put Dakota in the bedroom if we were running multiple errands or if it was possible for the errand to go longer than anticipated. You don't throw a child in the deep end of the pool without first making sure they can swim.

Once we knew we could trust her for a half hour, we upped it to one hour, then two. We started putting her in the bedroom when we went to the grocery store. We made sure not to combine errands during this phase of her training if in doing so she'd be left for longer than we felt she was ready for.

Little by little we left her in the bedroom for longer periods, always pottying her right before we left and again *immediately* when we got home. Our own personal potty could wait, putting up groceries could wait, everything could wait for us to take her out to pee because she was in a highly excited state. We'd take her out as fast as we could get her out the door, afterward giving her a really good treat and a lot of praise, and then all of us settling down to our normal routines.

Dakota quickly realized that when we left, we either put her in the crate or we put her in the bedroom. We'd estimate how long we'd be gone and then decide between the two. If she was up to two hours in the bedroom and we were just going to the grocery store, then it was a bedroom day, but if we were going to a friend's house for the evening, it meant we'd be gone for several hours so we put her in the crate. She had to work her way up to being left alone in the bedroom for that many hours.

Dakota fully understood that this was an option and that she didn't have to be in the crate when we left. As soon as she saw that we were going somewhere, she'd hightail it up the stairs and into the bedroom. She'd look at us with woeful eyes begging us to let her stay in the bedroom. It was hard. She knew that the bedroom was an option, so it was hard for us to put her in the crate. It felt like we were punishing her even though she hadn't done anything wrong.

Training her to be home alone was a critical step for a dog that came to us with so many problems. We didn't want to jump too far forward too fast in her training. We couldn't give her freedom for six hours until we knew she could handle two, then three, then four, then five. As hard as it was to look her in the eye and put her in the crate, we had to follow the plan diligently to ensure her success.

When we first adopted her I could not have imagined leaving her alone in the house for even one single minute. One year later she spent six hours alone in the bedroom while we were out and she aced it. I was so very proud of the progress she had made from being the most godawful dog, to this incredible dog that I was learning to trust. It took another year to give her full run of the house while we were gone though she did have run of the house when we were outside.

The long delay in training was primarily because we didn't want to leave her alone with Gypsy Rose. She never gained our trust in that area so we kept them separated if we were not around to supervise.

When we attempted to put Gypsy Rose in the bedroom and let Dakota have full run of the house, both dogs felt as if they were being punished. The bedroom was Dakota's safe place and she didn't like being locked out. For Gypsy Rose the bedroom felt like punishment, never having been so restricted before, so we aborted our efforts to give Dakota run of the house until Gypsy Rose passed away which was almost a year later.

Once Gypsy Rose passed away we started giving Dakota full run of the house just as we'd done with the bedroom — starting with short periods of time and then graduating to longer periods until we finally left her on a workday.

Today she routinely spends our workdays in the house without incident — no chewing, no potty, and no barking. We believe she spends most of the time snoozing in the bedroom — the room she has claimed for her safe haven. We don't even give it a thought anymore to worry about leaving her. We are so incredibly proud of her.

Interviewed for Victoria Stilwell

Good dog, bad dog
(Make up your mind!)

Once upon a time, Dakota would have been a prime candidate to meet Victoria Stilwell, master dog trainer in the television show *It's Me or the Dog*. One year after adopting Dakota, we were informally interviewed for the show.

We'd had a great day, my husband and I, out gallivanting in Marietta, Georgia, perusing the antique stores. We were hungry so we stopped for a bite to eat at a small, buffet-style restaurant.

In the next booth sat a man and woman talking about dogs. I heard the man talking about some folks they knew with a dog so awful that the owners were planning to get rid of the dog. The man was upset about their decision and he wanted to change their mind. This was clearly important to him.

We only caught bits and pieces of the conversation, but being smitten with our own saga of Dakota we couldn't help but eavesdrop. Humans tend to gravitate toward people who are sharing similar experiences, and what they were describing was a page straight out of Dakota's life story.

An embarrassing moment
(How to stick your foot in it)

We finished our meal and my husband went off to the restroom. I'd been debating through most of the meal whether to butt in and offer up the link to Dakota's online diary. I jotted down the website url on a slip of paper and handed it to the man, not expecting to talk to them, just giving a brief explanation of the Dakota articles as something that might help with this dog they were talking about.

By the time my husband came back from the restroom, I was immersed in a conversation with this man and woman. As it turned out, they were connected to Victoria Stilwell's dog training show, *It's Me Or The Dog*. I was in awe. What were the odds? Who could imagine meeting part of Victoria's team while we were out eating lunch — and what had I done? I had offered them dog training tips. Talk about embarrassing! Victoria was one of the most famous dog trainers with her own dog training show on television, and here I was giving advice? I was mortified but I kept on talking.

Is your dog bad enough?
(If she was still godawful she could have met Victoria)

Much to my surprise they were very interested in hearing about Dakota. I didn't realize that they were in the Atlanta area actively looking for bad dogs for the show. If you exhibit the slightest interest in hearing about Dakota, I'll talk for hours without much prodding, so I didn't wonder about their many questions. They were dog people and what dog person wouldn't want to hear about Dakota's multitude of sins? Like a proud parent I blathered on with every dirty tale I could think of.

I regaled them with how awful she'd been when we adopted her, and how her previous owners had gotten rid of her for being so awful. I told them how she'd peed on just about every square inch of our carpeting. I started to tell them her rolling in the poop story but stopped myself, realizing that these poor people were eating lunch. They didn't seem to care. They wanted more and they wanted the dirty details.

Did Dakota sleep in bed with us? Did we have any photos with us? Was she out in the truck right now? What breed was she? Did she have the beautiful blue eyes of the Siberian Husky? Did we ever argue about her? Did we know of anybody else with a bad dog?

Apparently they were shooting a season here in Atlanta and they needed five or six more problem dogs to feature.

Dakota was too good for them
(We'd done such a good job that she didn't need Victoria)

We know the show intimately. We'd watched every episode from the beginning, so we knew what sort of dogs got featured on the show. I told them that one year earlier, Dakota would have been the perfect candidate but today, she'd come so far in her training that she just wasn't bad enough to meet Victoria. At that very moment Dakota was home alone loose in the bedroom and we didn't anticipate any problems. They were disappointed. We had totally caught their interest with the stories of her first months with us.

I told them that I gave Victoria Stilwell a lot of credit for Dakota's progress, because some of the techniques I'd used with Dakota were learned from, *It's Me Or The Dog.*

My husband wanted to know what kind of car Victoria would be driving on the show. They weren't sure so they made a phone call to find out, and said it would be a Corvette.

They asked if we'd ever seen the television show *Dog Whisperer* and I said no, we didn't get that channel, but that we had watched *Good Dog U* and that for us, Victoria blew it right out of the water.

Can we meet Victoria Stilwell?
(Maybe if we pretend that Dakota is still bad?)

We would have loved to meet Victoria. She is one of our idols. Not only is she a genuinely talented dog trainer but she is also very entertaining and fun to watch. Unfortunately the show is taped in people's homes, not in a television studio, so you can't be part of a studio audience or go on set.

We were both deflated to miss out on Victoria, but at the same time it made me proud to know that Dakota had progressed to where she simply wasn't bad enough to meet Victoria Stilwell and be featured on her television show, *It's Me Or The Dog.* Dakota had made incredible progress on her journey.

After meeting the two folks who worked with Victoria, I looked her up on the internet. I was mostly interested in finding a reference to their seeking bad dogs for the show, but what I found was much more interesting — I found Victoria Stilwell's website.

Her list of credentials is mind boggling. She has worked with a large number of organizations on behalf of dogs. She has written books, given corporate seminars, and has even worked with our very own Paws Atlanta rescue shelter! Who knew that Victoria Stilwell was right around the corner from us, helping dogs just like Dakota?

Motivating Your Dog

Happy dogs are easier to train
(If a dog doesn't wanna, he isn't gonna)

What motivates you to do someone's bidding? A scowling face and the fear of something bad if you don't do the deed? Or a jovial atmosphere of fun and camaraderie? What sort of boss would you work the hardest for?

Spread the joy
(And your dog will reward you)

You've worked hard to retrain your dog and you're hoping that he will reward you with years of good behavior. You want him to be your best buddy. Maybe you've reached a stumbling block and you're wondering if there really is hope after all.

I've taken you through some of the worst moments we've had with our shelter dog Dakota when she peed all over the house, barked all day, chewed things, and bullied our other dog. Dakota came to us broken. She was wild and out of control and we had to invest a lot of hard work and patience to fix her. It wasn't a quick and easy fix. Retraining Dakota took time and perseverance, but we stuck with it and today we are reaping the rewards of a beloved companion.

Training, however, is just part of the equation. No amount of training can be successful if your dog doesn't want to obey you. If a dog doesn't wanna, he isn't gonna. One of the key factors in training a dog is to also focus on the happiness of the dog, and your relationship with him.

A happy dog will try harder to please you and obey your rules. A well adjusted dog will have fewer stress issues to cause bad dog behavior. Most used dogs are not well adjusted, even dogs who've never been in an animal shelter, but you can help them through some of the mental issues that manifest into bad behaviors. A dog whose family abandoned him, even when given directly to another family, can still experience abandonment stress. Dogs have no idea why their family suddenly disappeared. One day they had a family, and the next day their family and their home went poof, never to be seen again. Imagine how you'd react if a family member that lived in the same house with you simply disappeared forever without explanation, or if your very house was plucked out from underneath you.

Separation anxiety
(A used dog's biggest fear)

With any used dog, you are dealing with an abandoned dog and this can cause separation anxiety issues. Used dogs live in fear of being abandoned again — especially if you are yelling at them — and the fear is compounded for shelter dogs. If you put a shelter dog into an environment that reminds him of the shelter or that makes him feel alone — such as a garage or a far corner of the back yard — he will reward you with excessive barking, digging, or chewing. He might even develop the nervous habit of chewing on himself and causing bare spots on his skin. Used dogs are emotionally needy.

When we first put Dakota in the garage she barked all day. As soon as we brought her indoors into a dog crate, the barking stopped and we didn't have a problem with it again. The garage upset her, while the house made her feel safe. The crate solved some of our potty problems as well — though not all of them.

Man's best friend
(And how to be a best friend in return)

Dogs are meant to be Man's Best Friend and you wouldn't stick your best friend alone and forgotten somewhere. Most dogs do best by their owner's side as part of the family, so how should you treat your newest family member and keep him smiling?

One of Dakota's first happy moments was the potty treat. Once she got the hang of pottying outdoors we turned the treat into a game. She didn't get the treat immediately after doing the deed, but we did quickly bring her back indoors for the treat. If you wait too long, your dog may not associate the treat with the behavior that you are rewarding.

As soon as we were back in the house we played the game. She had to sit in the doorway — the same doorway where we'd trained her to wait for us to feed her — and then we'd toss the potty treat for her to catch. She got the treat, plus a game, and she learned the word *catch* in the process. Sometimes we changed the potty treats using dog biscuits or raw baby carrots to add a bit of diversity to her routine.

This was a fun moment in her day — something she looked forward to. Feeding time was also a fun game. We taught her to wait in the doorway for permission to enter. I often made a game of it and tested her at the same time. The release word was *okay* and sometimes I'd chatter off a string of other words before saying *okay*. She'd have to listen carefully for the magic word. I'd try to trick her with similar sounding words and phrases such as *Oklahoma* and *O Christmas tree*. We'd taught her to specifically wait for the word *okay* so she'd listen with anticipation, excitement, tail wagging and a happy dog face. Dakota had to listen and think.

This was mental stimulation which was just as valuable as physical stimulation for her. Once I said *okay* she'd come flying into the kitchen at full speed to her food bowl. Make learning fun and interesting and your dog will learn faster.

Dogs are pack animals
(They were not designed to be alone)

A dog is a pack animal. In the wild a dog does not live alone, he lives in a pack with several other dogs. They hunt together, sleep together, and entertain each other.

DAKOTA AND GYPSY ROSE ON A WALK TOGETHER

When a dog is abandoned by his people it goes against the very nature of being a dog. You are supposed to trust your pack. It throws a dog's psyche into turmoil for their pack to disappear without warning. One day they're surrounded by family — the next day *poof* — the family is gone. What happened? The dog has no idea.

Shelter dogs have abandonment fears. Their previous family let them down. Their trusted family took them to a cold, lonely place, left them there and never came back. Even a dog who has been given from one family directly to another will have the fear of losing their people. One day they had people — the next day those people were gone forever. You cannot expect a dog who was previously abandoned to trust in you, to trust that you'll be there tomorrow and next week and next month. You must build that trust, and it may take a year or two for the dog to finally believe that you won't abandon him as his previous owners did.

We are family
(The good, the bad, the ugly)

I acknowledged Dakota every time I walked past her unless she was sound asleep. If she was sitting, I'd reach out and touch her head gently as I walked past with just a brush of my hand. If she was laying down, I might bend down and touch her. Sometimes I'd just talk to her, or I'd simply look at her and smile. Dogs are able to read moods and emotions from our facial expressions just as we can read the moods and emotions of the people we see. Facial expressions send your dog messages just as strongly as words and actions do. Your dog will learn to recognize a scowl just as he'll learn to recognize a smile.

With every communication I was letting her know that she was part of a family now — not an abandoned dog. I'd tell her *you've got people*. It didn't matter if she understood the exact words; she heard the soft tone and took it as a happy message of some sort. Words don't always have to be about giving a command.

A tired dog is a good dog
(And a bored dog is a bad dog)

Dakota was a high energy dog — half Australian Cattle Dog and half Siberian Husky — two breeds accustomed to being

BAD DOG TO BEST FRIEND

on the move most of their waking hours. Ideally she needed rigorous exercise every day, as in a good run and not just a walk around the block. In a perfect world she'd have owners who could run next to her, or even skate or bike to allow her to truly run off all that energy, but it's not a perfect world.

Once we fenced the yard, we took her out for a game of fetch several times a week with us throwing the ball and Dakota running to retrieve it. This is great exercise for a dog and it doesn't wear the people out. Also, fencing the yard allowed her freedom to run every day to her heart's content, and she'd run and run and run, just for the love of running. I don't think any human alive could have kept pace with her.

One of our dog mantras was: *A tired dog is a good dog.* I can attest that this is the absolute truth. The more often we exercised Dakota outdoors, the fewer dog problems we had with her in general. It even carried over into subsequent days.

Sometimes we took her for a walk around the neighborhood to check out the world; other times we allowed her to sit on the upper deck where she could take in the sights and smells and sounds. Dakota had an eagle-eye view of the neighborhood from the upper deck and this was stimulation for her. It was also a break from boredom. Dogs get bored with the same old thing just as we do, and a bored dog is a bad dog.

Couch potatoes, there is hope even for you (Owner SITS while dog PLAYS)

Most of our evenings are spent indoors in front of the television. This is not particularly fun for an active dog, but there are things you can do to compensate. We played the *go find it* game almost every night — hiding treats and telling her to go find them. Sometimes we'd hide a single rawhide stick, and sometimes we'd hide several dog biscuit halves. Then we'd release Dakota from her *stay* position at the top of the stairs, tell her *go*

114

find it and she'd come flying down the stairs at top speed to search for the hidden treat with pure joy in every move. She loved this game. It had the added bonus of something to eat at the end and for Dakota, food had always been a big motivator.

When we first taught her the game, we had to help her along a bit and show her where some of the treats were hidden. She also watched our other dog and initially followed Gypsy Rose instead of looking on her own. It frustrated her to see Gypsy Rose finding so many goodies. Before long she figured out the *go find it* game and started sniffing around the room on her own looking for the hidden treats.

Some of the hiding places we chose were behind a table leg, behind a big chair, right up against the couch ruffle where it wasn't easily visible, under a throw rug, or on a windowsill.

Once the dogs had found all the treats we'd tell them *that's it, you found it* and give a hand signal to end the game. It didn't usually work and they'd sniff around a few more minutes before giving up the search. Eventually they'd flop down in happy relaxation. The game provided an adrenaline rush at the beginning and a treat at the end. They had to use their special dog talents to find the treat which was also stimulation for them.

How much is that doggie in the window? (And what makes that waggly tail?)

When we were at work, Dakota spent her time snoozing, looking out the window, pacing, or watching the door for our return. We actually verified this with a dog collar camera, though that was long after we'd successfully retrained her.

We had brought her to a place where we could trust her outside of the crate when we were gone. The stimulation we offered in the evening made up for some of the boredom of the day. We played fun dog games and gave her treats, making sure she had something to look forward to.

Even a small outing made a world of difference. Taking her out with me to check the mail — even though it only lasted a couple of minutes — broke up the boredom in her day. If she saw me at the front door holding the leash, she immediately knew we were going outdoors and her face would break into a happy dog grin with tail wagging and eyes shining bright. I'd put the leash on, take her around the side of the house to let her pee, then we'd go out to the mailbox and get the mail. It gave her a chance to sniff the air and look up and down the street.

Once we knew we could trust her not to pee in the car, we started bringing her along on errands that didn't involve leaving her in the car unattended. That's extremely dangerous, especially on a warm day. Dogs can die in a matter of minutes from being left in a hot car, even with the windows down, so we only took her on errands where she wouldn't be left alone.

If the errand was a trip to the bank's drive up window, or to pick someone up or drop them off, there was no reason she couldn't go. These were simple outings and yet they made all the difference to Dakota, adding joy to her day.

Every dog should have access to legal toys (Dog paraphernalia)

Our living room was littered with hard dog bones. If we weren't playing a game, Dakota would choose a bone to chew on. Rawhides were special treats stored in the dog closet, only to be brought out for brief periods. We didn't let her linger on the rawhides, watching carefully to make sure she didn't ingest too much. Ditto for hooves. In years past we used to leave hooves lying around, but the hooves that have been coming out lately tend to shatter so we stopped giving them to the dogs. They shatter into sharp pieces that can pierce a dog's innards and kill them. Plus we couldn't trust Dakota not to swallow a big chunk. It just isn't worth the risk.

Kong toys didn't make it. Dakota was an expert chewer and even the mighty Kong toys did not survive her teeth. Any plastic toy that she could pull pieces off of got quickly nixed as we didn't want her swallowing plastic.

In training to be the perfect dog
(And forgiving your best friend the occasional slip up)

Even the perfect dog can occasionally slip up. Our dog Gypsy Rose was literally the perfect dog. She was incredible. We trusted her alone in anybody's house or hotel room. We trusted her not to potty inside, ever. We trusted her not to chew on anything we hadn't given her, no matter what or where it was. We trusted her with children. Gypsy Rose was that good.

However, even Gypsy Rose had a couple of big baddies through the years that we forgave her for immediately. One year on New Year's Eve (long before Dakota came into our lives) we went to a party. We knew we'd be spending the night to avoid drinking and driving, so we put Gypsy Rose in the garage with some newspapers to potty on, a big watering jug, and a bowl full of food.

The neighbors shot off firecrackers right next to the garage and Gypsy Rose freaked out so badly that she chewed a huge chunk out of the door frame trying to get into the house. Gypsy Rose was petrified. Our dog who didn't chew things destroyed the door frame that night. We understood that the circumstances which caused her misbehavior were not normal, that mortal fear was driving her to seek out the safety of her home, and we took care not to leave her alone again on any holiday where people would shoot off firecrackers. Sometimes even the best behaved dog will have a bad moment.

Is Dakota perfect? Not by a long shot. She still gets into trouble but the nature of the trouble isn't as mission critical as it once was. I cannot remember the last time she peed in the house or destroyed something. Most of her trouble times are about not coming when we are in the back yard. We were so focused on solving the indoor problems, and on ensuring peace between the two dogs, that we did not work with her as diligently outdoors in those early months. The end result was that some of the bad outdoor behavior lingered.

Dakota has progressed to where we can leave her alone with full run of the house, take her on road trips, and she obeys most of our commands. She has learned a lot of words and she's great fun to have around. She's pretty amazing for a dog who came to us as the dog from hell.

Fun and Games

The Perfect Outdoor Dog Game
(Some games just weren't meant for Dakota)

Finding ways to entertain your dog can be challenging. Dakota was an energetic dog who needed a lot of exercise so we got her a big, bouncy ball about the size of a volleyball. We weren't the sort to go jogging or rollerblading so we looked for ways to exercise the dog without a lot of effort on our part.

This brilliant flash of inspiration came from a dog show on television where a dog was happily chasing a big rubber ball around the yard. The ball was too big for the dog to pick up in his teeth. All he could do was try to pounce on the ball and poke it with his nose while the ball scooted around the yard leading him on a merry chase. We were sold. Dakota got her first big rubber ball.

We set her loose to play with the ball fully expecting a hilarious show. The game lasted for all of one minute and we heard a *pop*. Dakota stopped dead in her tracks. She frowned and looked up at us with a big question mark on her face. *Huh? What's sort of toy is this?* The ball flew off in a big whoosh till it was flat as a pancake and then it dropped to the ground. Dakota poked her nose at it a couple times to see if it would magically reanimate and roll off for a new game, but the flattened ball just laid there, totally inert.

It must have taken a supreme effort for Dakota to open her jaws wide enough to puncture that ball. Our dog with teeth like a shark and the burning desire to chew didn't give up until she had succeeded in sinking her teeth into the ball. Apparently the television dogs played nice with their toys.

I would have chalked it up to a grand $3 experiment but my husband decided that the ball was defective. It had a picture of a dog on it so surely it should have lasted more than a minute with our dog. He took it back to the store. The store clerk asked the reason for the return. He told her that it hadn't lasted even five minutes with the grandkids and he wanted his $3 back. The clerk looked closely at the ball and said, "My, what big teeth your grandchildren have!" She looked him straight in the eye but she did give the $3 back.

We eventually found a ball that lasted much longer. It's some sort of soccer ball and even though she can pick it up with her teeth, it doesn't burst. She can entertain herself until she finally wears herself out. We don't even have to lift a finger. She throws it, catches it, shakes it, chases it, and pounces on it, all without any input from us.

Dakota also has a tennis ball for fetch games and we have a ball thrower so we can really wing it. She'll fetch a couple times but she'd rather just run with the ball in her mouth so she can chew on it while running. She knows we'll take it away if she lays down with it because she'll chew on it until there's nothing left. We can't get mad because it is her toy. We worked pretty hard to find ways for her to use her teeth legally so she wouldn't gnaw on our furniture, shoes, and so forth, and our efforts have paid off.

Give Your Dog Something to Think About

A bored dog is a bad dog
(Nothing to do but think up ways to get in trouble)

It's common knowledge that dogs need physical exercise, but did you know that your dog also needs mental stimulation? Dogs are highly intelligent beings. Their minds are active just as ours are, and they spend time thinking about things just as we do. If you don't give your dog constructive things to think about, you can bet that he's still thinking about something and you probably won't like the result.

A bored dog will think of ways to amuse himself such as chewing, barking, or chasing the cat. He may try to figure out ways to scoot through the front door and out into the interesting world. He may go poking his nose where it doesn't belong such as the garbage can or your shoe closet. He may find you boring and simply ignore you.

You can give your dog positive things to think about. Teaching your dog basic commands is a good place to start, but you can also teach him other words. Dogs have the ability to learn a large vocabulary of words and phrases. The more words your dog knows, the more time he will spend listening to everything you say even if you're not talking to him. Your dog will be listening for words that he understands. This not only strengthens the bond between you and your dog, it also keeps his mind from wandering down the forbidden trails.

Teaching your dog new words is much like teaching a child. Every time he encounters an object such as a ball, you say a word for him to associate with that object. You can teach your dog specific food words as well. Before long he will know words for many objects and types of food — for example: ball, toy, bone, water, frisbee, stick, teddy bear, blanket, chewie, bed, crate or house, hot dog, peanut butter, carrot, cheese, and virtually any other object or food he encounters.

Say it again, Sam
(I didn't hear you the first time)

The first time you try to teach your dog a new word he will cock his head and look puzzled. He is trying to understand you and he will think hard to accomplish that goal. Be repetitive. Show him the ball and say *ball*. Before long you'll be able to tell him to *go get the ball* and he will. When he accomplishes the task successfully, make sure to praise him.

Mix it up a little. Teach him different words for all of his toys so that he will know the difference between *go get the ball* and *go get the frisbee*. Once Dakota had learned the *go find it* game in the house, we could then use the *go find it* command outdoors. If we were playing fetch with the ball in the back yard and she didn't see where the ball went we could say, *"Go find it! Go find the ball!"* and she would immediately go in search of the ball, searching the entire back yard including the wooded areas on each side. This added a second game to the first: (1) chasing after and retrieving the ball, and (2) searching for a lost ball.

EAGER TO LEARN

Words are powerful tools in your arsenal. In addition to providing mental stimulation, words strengthen the bond between you and your dog. Every time you give your dog a treat, give the treat a name as you hand it to him and be specific. What kind of treat is it? Your dog has the ability to learn different words or phrases such as cheese, broccoli, cabbage, peanut butter, bacon, Milk Bone, or pig ear. Broccoli and cabbage? Yes, some dogs enjoy broccoli stems and cabbage hearts. If you cut the head off of your broccoli and throw the stem away, instead give the stem to your dog as a treat.

Can't I just have it?
(Pretty please? I'll be so cute for you)

Make your dog work for his treats. Never give him a treat just because he's staring at you with big, woebegone eyes. Ask your dog to do a trick or a series of tricks before you give him the treat, or make him catch the treat as you toss it to him. Your goal is to give your dog things to think about.

Challenge your dog to think by making a game out of giving him the treat. Let your dog choose which treat he wants. Put five different treats on the floor spaced about a foot apart. Whichever treat he chooses, put the others away. The more mental stimulation you provide, the less opportunity your dog has to think of bad things.

The next set of words and phrases is a bit more complex. They involve specific actions. Here are a few examples and ways you can teach your dog to understand them.

Go to bed: If your dog has a bed, lead him to it and say *go to bed*. If he leaves the bed, lead him back to the bed. It may take a week or so before your dog learns the phrase but if you are persistent, he will learn it. Always say *good dog* when he successfully follows the command. Dogs respond well to positive praise. Follow it up with a food treat and he will learn it even faster. Food is a powerful motivator.

Catch: Throw a piece of food near his head and say *catch*. At first he'll watch the food whiz past. He will investigate, then eat the food and look to you with interest. Games that involve food get their attention. Throw another piece while saying *catch*. If your dog snatches it in midair, make a big deal out of his being a good dog and repeat the action. He will learn *catch* in record time with a food treat coupled with a cheerful *good dog*.

Potty, pee pee, or poopie: Every time you take your dog out for potty, say the word *potty*. If he pees, say *pee pee* and if he poops, say *poopie*. Repeat this every time you take him out and he will catch on quickly. Dogs are fully able to differentiate between the two and if he knows these words, you'll be able to tell him do a specific deed on command. This is useful if you're on a road trip and need your dog to do his business on command at rest stops.

If you're on a road trip and your dog hasn't peed in awhile I can guarantee there's business that can be done on command.

Don't make the mistake of assuming he doesn't need to go pee just because he didn't immediately do the deed. If it's been awhile and he knows the command *pee pee*, be persistent so that you can be absolutely sure that he's empty before the trip resumes. You don't want another voice clamoring to stop for a bathroom. Tell him *good dog* for a potty well done in your happy dog voice. Dogs respond to your tone of voice just as they respond to the words.

Move: Not only is this command useful for making your dog move out of your way, it also helps establish your position as alpha dog. If your dog is snoozing in the doorway and you step over him, you're telling him that he is the alpha dog. Instead, gently move him out of your way and say *move*. At first you'll need to rouse him from his comfy position every time you pass through the doorway. Don't forget to say *good dog* in your happy voice when he's out of the doorway, even if you moved him out.

Initially your dog will resist. This is a battle for alpha dog positioning and it's serious business. Be persistent; don't let him woo you with his big, puppy dog eyes and he'll get the message. Soon you'll be able to say *move* as you approach the doorway and he will automatically get up and move out of your way. He may even move before you give the command when he sees you approach, this being the epitome of success.

Turn Around or Circle: Teach your dog to turn around in a circle. Holding a piece of food at nose level, lead him in a tight circle while saying *turn around*. It's a rare dog who won't follow that piece of food. At first, his focus will be on the food and the words will get lost in the shuffle. After a few times try it without the food and just use your finger to lead him in a circle. If successful, give him the food treat and tell him *good dog*. Eventually you'll be able to say *turn around* without even being near your dog and he'll do it.

Shake: Not only can your dog learn to shake hands, he can learn to do it with either his right or left paw. With your dog in a

125

sitting position, take his paw and shake hands while saying the word *shake*. After showing him a few times, try just reaching your hand out, palm up in front of the foot you want him to shake with. If he lifts his paw tell him *good dog*, grab his paw and shake hands with him. Soon he will be putting his paw in your hand on command, and then you can move to the next phase.

Other Foot: Now try it with the opposite foot, giving that foot a different word or phrase such as *other foot*. Use your other hand to correspond with his other foot. When your dog gets good at it you can make a game out of switching feet. You can even give this command from a distance to teach him to raise a paw. Your challenge will be to get him to *stay* where he is and not come toward you.

Other Side: If he is on one side of you, gently guide him to your other side while saying *other side*. Why would you want to teach him this? Your dog may be on the wrong side when you're opening a door. If you have a drink in your hand, you might want him on your other side. You probably don't want him between you and the stair railing if you're going up or down the stairs. Every word you teach your dog is a good word and sooner or later it will come in handy.

Get Behind Me: Move the dog behind you while saying the phrase until he gets the hang of it. Dogs prefer to take the lead so you'll need to be very persistent. This is useful when opening doors or walking through narrow hallways.

Wanna Go For A Ride? If you take your dog for car rides he will love learning this one. Repeat the phrase every time he gets in the car and before long, you'll be able to say it before you even leave the house and your dog will get excited. You can do the same with *wanna go for a walk* or *wanna go out*. Dogs are very intelligent. You can choose whatever word or phrase works best for you. *Wanna go for a walk* can just as easily be *go for a walk* or just *walk*. However, using a phrase rather than a single word makes it easier to use the same word in different phrases. For example, you might prefer to say *walk with me* instead of *heel*. You can then use the word *walk* in two different phrases and he will learn to differentiate between the two.

Go Up: Guide him up the stairs while saying *go up*. Reward your dog at the top of the stairs. You might prefer *go upstairs* or just *up*. It doesn't matter which words you use as long as you are consistent and use the same word or phrase every time. There are no magic words when training a dog. The words can be whatever you wish including words in a different language such as German, French, or Spanish.

You can also teach your dog sign language. This doesn't mean you need to learn sign language for the deaf. It simply means that you can teach your dog a hand signal that represents a command.

Moving your finger in a circle can be your sign for *turn around*. Holding your hand up in the stop position can accompany the command *stay*. Pointing your finger at the ground is a good hand signal for *lie down*. *Come*, *go away*, *move*, *sit*, and *speak* can all have hand signals in addition to voice commands.

The hand signal itself does not matter. As long as you use it consistently, your dog can learn it. Simply use the signal every time you give the verbal command and he will learn to associate the hand signal with the action. Eventually you'll be able to use the hand signal without any words.

A fun game to play with your dog after he has learned a few hand signals is to give him a series of commands with hand signals only. He can sit, lie down, turn around, speak, and shake hands without you ever saying a word. It's a fun game and it gives your dog something to think about. If he loses his hearing as he gets older, you'll have an alternative form of communication.

Everything you teach your dog exercises his brain. Not only are you teaching him to listen to your every word, he must also watch your hands for messages. He is thinking about the things you have taught him and that's what you want. He'll have less time to think about getting in trouble. Even when your dog appears to be snoozing there's a good chance he is listening to you talk to people in the room or on the phone. The next time you use a word that he knows during regular conversations with people, watch his ears perk up.

Make a habit of talking to your dog even when you're not giving a command. He doesn't need to understand everything you say. Talking to him often will let him know he is not alone, and that he will need to listen in case you're saying words that he understands. If you've taught him the word *window* when you are opening the blinds, then the next time you open the blinds in another room you can casually tell him you opened his window. He'll pick up on the word *window* in the sentence. If he is bored he might decide to investigate.

As you walk past, tell him *we're buddies* or *what a pretty dog*. It doesn't matter whether he understands or not. He will listen to the words and think about them. The communication will strengthen your bond with him.

Games, oh boy!
(Dogs are like children, they need lots of play)

Your dog's vocabulary can help you play games with him. Games offer another form of mental stimulation, especially games that make your dog think. The *go find it* game is a good example. Hide a dog treat and teach your dog to go find it. At first he won't understand. You'll need to guide him to the treat while saying *go find it*. Next time, hide the treat in a different place. Before long he will associate the words *go find it* with a hidden treat that he must look for. In the beginning, choose easy locations such as behind a chair leg or in a corner. Once he gets the hang of it you can be more creative. Hide the treat in a hollow dog bone, under a rug, behind a door, or even in another room if he gets too good at searching one room.

If your dog knows other commands you can make them part of the game as well. Send your dog *upstairs* and tell him to *stay* while you hide the treat downstairs. Now he has several things to think about before the game even begins. *Go upstairs*, *stay*, and then *go find it*. Don't let him come down the stairs before you are ready. Shoo him back up the stairs and make sure he waits for the release word such as *okay*.

Turn around, *catch*, *other foot*, and *shake* make great tricks to show off for visitors and you can give your dog a series of commands before giving him a treat. He will be overjoyed to put on a show. Dogs are not only intelligent, some are highly social. Any chance you give your dog to interact with you will help to fill their thoughts and their time so that they don't go looking for negative ways to amuse themselves.

Teaching your dog new words and new games is not only fun for the dog, it provides mental stimulation. You are giving him fun things to think about. Your dog will spend his time listening to you, watching you, and waiting for the next fun game. Just remember one phrase: *A bored dog is a bad dog.* Give your dog fun things to think about and make games a part of his normal routine. He will reward you by being a much happier dog who gets into a lot less trouble.

Challenge for Alpha

So you think you're the boss?
(Maybe you were yesterday, but today is a
brand new day)

Dakota had been progressing. From her early days with us as the most godawful dog imaginable, she had reached a place where she brought us joy and laughter rather than hard work and frustration. She'd come a long way from the early days of peeing all over the house, chewing, picking on our other dog, and escaping into the wild blue yonders.

After two years of hard work, Dakota brought laughter into the house instead of *Don't Kill the Dog* sticky notes. Most of her problems had been solved.

Dakota was a happy dog. She was also a very strong-willed dog. Dakota was not only born to be an alpha dog, her formative months without any sort of training had empowered that aspect of her personality.

Our other dog, Gypsy Rose, passed away at fifteen years old, and Dakota surprised us by not sniffing around for the missing pack member. She now had our full attention and she was loving it. The competitor was gone and Dakota was happy for about two weeks, until she unexpectedly reverted to some of her earlier bad behavior. She'd been doing so well, why was she suddenly being bad?

For example, I would let her out for potty and she wouldn't come back in. At first she'd linger just a little longer than usual, then longer and longer until she simply refused to come when called, pointedly blowing me off with her body language. Things came to a head one morning when I was late for work because she decided to gallivant for 45 minutes. I had to revisit some of the training methods I'd used to deal with it before.

But the question haunted me: *why was she acting up?* Why was Dakota suddenly being such a bratty dog? I'd been so proud of her, and now here she was being awful again. *Why?*

Then it hit me. We'd lost a pack member — a senior member who'd been in the pack for many years before Dakota joined us. This was Dakota's perfect opportunity to challenge for pack leadership and that's exactly what she was doing — she was challenging me for the role of Leader of the Pack.

In the dog world, pack leaders don't get to sit on their laurels as an unchallenged dictator. Periodically the lesser dogs will challenge them for the role. Sometimes the lesser dog prevails and a new pack leader emerges from the fray. By the same token, your dog may periodically challenge your authority to make the rules. This is normal. Just revisit the training methods you originally used and stay firm. Put your foot down and don't let him get away with it. Eventually he will give up the challenge and life will go back to its happy place, for awhile anyways — at least until the next alpha challenge.

MERLE PATTERNED COAT

The Challenges of Owning an Ausky Dog

Dakota is an Ausky dog
(Which brought challenges of its own)

Every dog breed brings a unique set of challenges for the dog owner, and Auskies will provide more of a challenge than most. Be prepared for double the trouble if you decide to adopt an Ausky dog. Auskies are a mix of two strong-willed, independent dog breeds: Australian Cattle Dog (not to be confused with the Australian Shepherd) and Siberian Husky.

Both the Australian Cattle Dog (also known as an ACD, Blue Heeler, Red Heeler, Queensland Heeler, or just Heeler) and the Siberian Husky were bred to adapt to rough environments, run for hours on end, and make decisions independent of their owners.

Mix the two breeds together and the result is an intelligent, high energy, rough and tumble dog who will not readily give up control to an unprepared dog owner.

Get ready for a wild ride because here's what you can expect from your Ausky dog:

The Dog Who Was Born to Run

Australian Cattle Dogs were bred to control entire herds of cattle on the open range with minimal human input. To accomplish this, Cattle dogs are constantly on the move circling, running and guiding the cattle in the desired direction. Siberian Huskies were bred to run long distances while pulling sleds loaded with supplies and people.

BORN TO RUN

Two dogs that were bred for hard work, endurance, stamina, and staying on the move all day require an intense level of exercise. It's not enough to take your Ausky dog for a leisurely walk around the block. Auskies need to run fast and hard. This dog needs an owner with an active lifestyle. Jogging, hiking, and biking are excellent outlets for an energetic dog. Ausky dogs have the stamina to run for miles with you.

However, you should never run your Ausky dog off leash. Siberian Huskies do not possess the homing instinct inherent in many dog breeds, and they have a strong wanderlust. Your Ausky's love for the run can take him many miles from home before he realizes he's left you far behind. Once lost, he may not be able to find you again. It is strongly recommended that you microchip your Ausky.

At home, plan for a large, fenced yard, and games that encourage your Ausky dog to run, such as fetching a ball or frisbee.

This Dog Is One Smart Cookie

Siberian Huskies are considered to have average intelligence, while Australian Cattle Dogs are one the more intelligent breeds according to Stanley Coren in his book, *The Intelligence of Dogs*.

What high intelligence means to you as a dog owner is that your dog will be thirsty for knowledge. Fulfill that need and you will be rewarded for life. Ignore it at your own peril. A bored dog is likely to cause you a lot of trouble.

One of the hallmarks of the Australian Cattle Dog is the ability to think for themselves and make decisions independently of you. The ACD is an independent thinker — capable of doing a job without supervision — and he has the ability to solve complex problems. You will need to give this dog something to think about.

Teach him as many words and phrases as you can. Take his vocabulary far beyond the basic commands of *sit, stay, lay down, heel*, and so forth. Teach your dog words for specific objects, different types of food, and various actions. Play thinking games with your Ausky such as hiding a treat and making him search for it. Build an agility course in your back yard and teach him action words such as *up, down, jump*, and *tunnel*.

Create puzzles for your dog to solve. A company in Sweden called *Zoo Active Products* produces a variety of problem solving puzzles for dogs. Their website at nina-ottosson.com lists pet shops around the world where you can buy these puzzles. A search for "Nina Ottosson" on the internet will also bring up companies that sell her dog puzzles.

Ho Hum Boredom

Both Australian Cattle Dogs and Siberian Huskies are accustomed to new experiences and variety in their surroundings. Running the wilds of Alaska, Siberia, and Australia brings new sights, smells, sounds, and even flavors to the dogs lucky enough to enjoy such freedom. Your Ausky dog won't expect any less from his environment. If you don't provide fun activities to keep him busy and new experiences to spice up his life, your Ausky dog will find his own outlets for adventure and you probably won't like the results.

Do not let your Ausky get bored. Play games with him, indoors and out. Teach him dog agility, flyball, and tracking. Include him in as many family activities as possible. Take him on road trips, to the beach, or even just around town if at all possible. Do not, however, leave him unattended in the car.

Boredom can be tackled in small ways as well, such as letting your Ausky dog tag along on a trip to the mailbox. Once he knows the routine, he'll dance with joy when he sees the leash even if the outing only lasts for two minutes.

Tackling boredom in a dog doesn't necessarily mean you must keep him busy every waking moment. If you provide a variety of activities and outings that he can look forward to every day, you'll go a long way in fulfilling his need for adventure and prevent him from becoming a problem dog. In return, your Ausky dog will keep you laughing at his many antics. He will embrace virtually any game, often adding his own twist to the game rules. Expect the unexpected. This is a quirky dog full of spunk, spirit, and rollicking fun.

Houdinis of the Dog World

Why is it so important to keep your Ausky from getting bored? You don't want him to go looking for adventure on his own. Siberian Huskies are skillful escape artists. If they want the freedom to go chasing after adventure, they will find a way to get it. They are called *Houdinis of the Dog World* and for good reason.

Siberian Huskies have been known to escape from crates without opening the door, simply by squeezing their way out through the corners. Huskies will figure out how to unlatch doors and gates, both inside your home and outside. They will dig under fences or climb over chain link fences and stone walls. Huskies will even climb over wooden fences if there's a tree nearby to brace against as they shimmy their way upward.

Australian Cattle Dogs have their own methods of escape. They will happily chew through a rope or tie-down. They have been known to jump over, and even body slam fences — breaking the fence boards. Both breeds are undeterred by electric fences.

Your Ausky dog has the intelligence of the Australian Cattle Dog coupled with the Houdini spirit of the Husky. For every escape route that you close off, the Ausky will find or create two more. This is a breed that can slip out of collars and harnesses in the time it takes you to look away and back again. Unless he is very well trained, you cannot walk this dog and lose yourself in the scenery — you absolutely must keep one eye on your Ausky dog at all times.

Providing your Ausky with regular activities and adventures to look forward to will keep him from wanting to escape in search of his own adventures.

Dog Chewing, Digging, and Destructiveness

If he can't get enough fun and adventure in his life, your Ausky might resort to activities of a more destructive nature such as chewing and digging, traits that are pronounced in the two breeds that he sprang from.

Australian Cattle Dogs are mouthy dogs with an intense need to chew. It is imperative to direct this need to chew by giving them legal chew toys such as big rawhide bones. If you don't, they will find something else to chew on, and these dogs can be incredible engines of destruction. Teach your Ausky dog from an early age which items he can chew on. If you catch him chewing on something illegal, always replace it with a legal chew toy so that he learns which is which. By practicing due diligence in your dog training, you can steer his chewing habits into a more positive direction.

Keep in mind that most dog toys will not last long with an Australian Cattle Dog. It takes a tough toy to stand up to the intense chewing of this breed. Kong toys and Boomer Balls have the best chance of survival, but even Kong toys may need to be replaced on occasion. Better the toy than your house!

Siberian Huskies have their own path to destruction: they love to dig. This trait is inherent in the breed as they learned to dig nests in the snow in order to stay warm. Hunkering down in a dugout protects these snow dogs from the freezing Arctic winds.

Indoors your dog can dig a hole in the carpet, while outdoors your Ausky might turn his attention to your manicured lawn and flower beds if you don't redirect his need to dig. Give your Ausky his own sandbox to dig in and bury a few of his favorite toys to entice him. Create a legal place for him to dig or provide him with other outdoor activities such as games with the family, so that he forgets that he wants to dig.

Don't let your Ausky get bored. Provide him with activities and adventures as part of his daily routine, and you'll go a long way toward preventing him from ripping a path of destruction through your home and garden. Know what your dog was bred to do and find legal ways for him to fulfill those tendencies.

People Dogs

Time with the family is critical for your Ausky. This is a dog that needs to be close to you. An Ausky kept outdoors will become frustrated and troublesome for both you and your neighbors. He needs to live with you — indoors.

ARE YOU COMING?

The Australian Cattle Dog is often called a Velcro dog because you will become the center of his universe, and he will want to stay close to you. The worst fate you can bestow on an Australian Cattle Dog is to force him to live outdoors away from you. This is a dog who needs a lot of interaction with his human family. However, ACDs do not bond equally with all family members, usually choosing just one or two people to bestow their adoration upon.

AUSTRALIAN CATTLE DOG - SIBERIAN HUSKY MIX

Huskies are a bit more gregarious. They prefer the company of many people and many dogs and do best in multi-dog households. Siberian Huskies are people dogs. They will lavish their affection on anyone and everyone, including total strangers.

Neither breed does well when kept away from his people. Be prepared for your Ausky to become an integral part of your life. Look for ways to include him in your daily activities and consider taking him on vacations with you. Dog friendly vacations fulfill the need for adventure that accompanies both breeds. This is a dog who would love to take road trips with you. The trick is in planning a vacation that includes a big dog.

Trips to visit family and friends are a good place to start if you've trained your Ausky to play nice in the house. Dog friendly hotels open up many possibilities if your trip is primarily for outdoor adventures. A beach vacation is a good bet while a trip to Las Vegas wouldn't have much to offer a dog. Be aware that not all beaches and parks allow dogs, so do your homework first.

Nipping, Biting, and the Body Slam

The flip side of your people dog is that he's not always good with people. You'll need to keep a tight rein on your Ausky, especially around kids. Another quirk for the Australian Cattle Dog is a tendency to nip and body slam.

Think about it. How does a 60 pound dog control an entire herd of cattle weighing 1500 pounds each? It takes a dog with a lot of pluck to face off with an animal 25 times his size, and that's what a good Australian Cattle Dog will do, face off and stare down even the mightiest of cows.

However, the face off isn't always enough to keep a herd of cattle in line and the Australian Cattle Dog has quite a few tricks up his sleeve. His second line of offense to move a stubborn cow is the nip and run tactic. The Australian Cattle Dog will run in fast staying low to the ground, nip at the heels of the errant cow, and then quickly dart away before the cow can kick at him. That is the very definition of a heeler: "a dog that herds cattle by nipping or biting at their heels." The goal isn't to bite the cow hard enough to cause injury, it's simply to nudge the cow to start moving in a different direction than the cow wants to go.

When that fails, the dog has to bring out the big artillery — the body slam. Many an Australian Cattle Dog has injured himself throwing his body into a cow at full force in order to convince the cow to get a move on. Body slamming is serious business and it's the very nature of an ACD to body slam.

If you happen to be the target, more pity to you because it HURTS. A 60 pound mass of solid muscle charging into you at full speed will knock you for quite a loop. Cattle dogs don't mean to cause you harm, but nipping and body slams are simply what they were bred to do and you better be prepared for it.

Australian Cattle Dogs will make a great game of playing chicken with you, running circles around you at full speed, inching closer and closer as they whiz past trying to see how close they can actually get without slamming into you. Occasionally they'll miscalculate and slam you hard to the ground, afterwards looking at you with an innocent apology of, *"Oh sorry mate, I nicked you a bit, didn't I?"*

The body slam is hard to control when he's running at top speed toward you. Until you've trained him *not* to slam into you, the safest thing you can do is stand next to a tree when he goes into high gear. He'll veer off when a tree is involved.

Nipping is the other trait to be prepared for. You need to provide legal outlets for your dog's need to use his teeth. Australian Cattle Dogs are a very mouthy breed and will often gently chew on you as a sign of affection. If you teach him a word or phrase that means to stop chewing on you, it allows him to fulfill his affections for you within limits. However, you must teach him from the time he's a young pup that nipping at other people is not okay — even if just in play. Your visitors will not likely embrace this aspect of your dog and contrary to what many dog owners do, it's okay to put your dog away from guests if your visitors aren't dog people and your dog bothers them.

If you've made it this far, you're wondering why on earth anyone would want to adopt an Ausky dog. A breed that incorporates the best and worst of two breeds with a lot of quirks, Auskies present a serious challenge. However, the joy, laughter, and love they will bring into your life far outweighs the challenges if you have what it takes to work with an Ausky dog, and a lifestyle that suits their needs.

Whatever the activity, Auskies will do it with gusto. Even an activity as simple as drinking from the water dish is amusing for you as the dog owner — your Ausky will drink with such exuberance that you can hear water splashing even from a different room.

No activity is too mundane for the Ausky dog. They find ways to turn even the simplest activity into great fun, and their joy is contagious. Auskies love to clown around and it's hard to resist their goofy antics. This is a dog who can bring laughter to the most frustrating day and light up your loneliness with love.

If you live a very active lifestyle, your Ausky has the desire and stamina to share it with you — if you let him.

Watch Dog

Don't expect much in this department. Australian Cattle Dogs were bred to work in silence. Siberian Huskies will howl at sirens and make you laugh at their plethora of strange moans and sighs, but they are not known to be barkers. Your Siberian Husky may even shriek if forced to obey a command that he doesn't want to obey. Neither breed is likely to bark much unless he is very unhappy, such as when you force him to live outdoors or in a garage.

In addition, Siberian Huskies can sometimes be a little too welcoming of strangers. A stranger is simply a friend they haven't met before. Huskies are not bred for aggressiveness, though any dog can become so.

Australian Cattle Dogs are a bit more suspicious of strangers and have a stronger protective instinct. However, it takes a bit of training to convince your Ausky to bark when someone comes to the door, or is lurking outside the window.

Your best deterrent to burglars is that your Ausky will likely instill fear simply for his size and aggressive appearance. If a burglar does decide to take his chances, the Australian Cattle Dog's tendency to bite and body slam might change his mind in a hurry. A typical ACD body shove as the burglar is attempting to go up or down the stairs will likely cement the deal, sending the burglar scurrying out of your house as quickly as he can get out the door.

Rough and Tumble Dog

While the body slam might knock you for a loop, your Ausky might pause in his play for a bit but otherwise he'll be unperturbed. Chalk it up to his Australian Cattle Dog genes. Even though he's a lot smaller than you and can easily be injured during the body slam, your Ausky will ignore the pain, pushing on through whatever activity he is engaged in.

This is a dog who plays hard and often injures himself in the process. While his ability to dodge the hooves of a kicking cow usually serves him well, even the most experienced herding dog will occasionally get knocked around by 1500 pounds of irritable cow, and he was bred to bully his way through the pain and stay on the job.

Combine an agile dog who is built for endurance, with the love for the run, and you get a dog who'll entertain you outdoors with figure eights performed at top speeds as he cuts corners so tightly that he's almost laying down — eventually wiping out in a great ball of dust. A bruise here and there doesn't faze him —so expect a dog who bangs himself up, but don't trust him to tell you when a visit to the vet is in order. Use your own judgement when he sustains an injury.

Strong-Willed Dog

His tolerance for injury and his single-minded ability to face off with a 1500 pound cow affects the type of training that works best for your Ausky. A tough approach usually fails. Remember, he was bred to fight force with force so a heavy handed approach will bring out the stubbornness in him. You'll need to take a more positive approach when training this dog.

Your Ausky is the combination of two very strong-willed dogs, and training an Ausky is not for an inexperienced dog owner. Consider the breeds that went into your Ausky. Siberian

Huskies are a dominant, stubborn breed of dog. If you do not take a strong leadership role, they will not obey you. You must be a strong pack leader. If you don't take the role, your Husky will.

Ditto for Australian Cattle Dogs. They will not tolerate living in a pack without a strong leader, and if you don't take the role, they will. Two strong-willed breeds beget a dog that isn't suitable for an inexperienced dog owner. Be prepared to take your role as leader of the pack and the dogs will follow along, for the moment.

This does not mean that you should inflict harsh punishments for misbehavior. You will cause more problems with your Ausky by taking that route. Neither the Husky nor the Australian Cattle Dog respond well to harsh treatment. You'll fare much better with positive motivation and strong leadership.

Attempting to bully an Australian Cattle Dog will almost always backfire. Remember, Australian Cattle Dogs are bred to stand up to the full force of an angry cow. If the cow is disobedient and tries to kick the dog away, the ACD knows to pull a bigger trick out of his arsenal such as nipping or the body slam. He's not likely to respond to you any differently. You need to learn to make him want to obey, which is not an easy task.

The role of alpha dog means that you can be trusted to take care of, and make decisions for the pack. You can be trusted to rule the pack with fairness and consistency, to make sure the pack is fed and watered, and most of all, as alpha dog you are in charge of finding entertainment for the pack. Allowing the pack to entertain themselves opens up your household to all manner of dog destruction issues.

Both breeds will constantly push the boundaries, testing you to see how much they can get away with. They will challenge your authority and if they discover that you are a softie, you better watch out.

The Siberian Husky has a mind of his own and will obey on his own terms. Even if he fully understands a command, it's not uncommon for a Husky to simply decide he doesn't wanna if he hasn't embraced you as his leader. You must earn his respect if you have any hope for obedience.

The Australian Cattle Dog complicates it even further. More often than not he will accept only one person as boss. Everyone else in the family is considered lesser or equal, which means that your dog will only obey the secondary family members at his convenience, giving you quite a training challenge.

If you aren't prepared, both Huskies and Australian Cattle Dogs will teach you to do tricks for them, rather than vice versa. Even if you've successfully trained your Ausky, he will periodically challenge your authority over him, so be prepared to reinforce your alpha status throughout his lifetime.

Auskies and Kids

Because the Ausky needs a strong alpha leader, you shouldn't trust him to be walked by your kids. This is a recipe for disaster. Once he realizes that a lesser pack member is attempting to control him, he may seize the opportunity to cut loose.

Auskies are not the best dog to have around kids for a number of reasons. While Huskies tend to be gentle dogs, Australian Cattle Dogs are usually too rough to leave alone with smaller children, and they should *never* be allowed to run loose in the neighborhood.

If your Ausky has strong heeler traits, he will chase after kids who are running and nip at their heels and hands. You must teach any child who will spend time around your Ausky not to tease or pick on the dog. This should be a rule for any dog, but even more so with any type of cattle dog mix.

Your Ausky will fall somewhere in between the gentleness of the Husky and the roughness of the Australian Cattle Dog and you need to watch very carefully to see which way the winds blow before putting your trust in him around children.

Auskies and the Chase

Both Siberian Huskies and Australian Cattle Dogs have a strong predatory drive which makes them more likely to chase small animals, running children, and even cars. They will skillfully hunt down squirrels, rabbits, and birds. They will also hunt down your favorite pet hamsters and cats unless they've been raised to accept the other pet as part of their pack. Neighborhood cats, however, are fair game and if you're not careful, you could have a cat killer on your hands.

The instinct to herd and the instinct to chase are so strong that children who are running or bicycling are prime targets for an Ausky. A child who doesn't obey the Ausky's attempts to control him will be greeted with teeth or a body slam as the Ausky tries to control the child as he would a cow. Don't put your Ausky in this position and risk a lawsuit, or be forced to put him down for biting a child or killing a cat.

Another danger is chasing cars. To an Ausky, a car is simply a huge animal to chase down. They simply do not understand that cars are not cattle and cannot be controlled, herded, or caught, and the results are usually unfortunate for the dog who tries. Protect your Ausky — unless he's in your fenced yard, he should be on a leash.

Protecting your Ausky is only half the battle, however. You also need to fulfill his need for the chase in a legal way. Chasing a ball or frisbee is a good place to start. Fulfill his need to herd with a Boomer Ball. He can chase it around but he cannot pick it up or chew on it.

Auskies and Other Dogs

Huskies are good with other dogs if they are raised together from puppyhood. This is a breed of dog who prefers to have other dogs around and does well in a pack. Huskies are also friendly with strange dogs. Australian Cattle Dogs require a bit more work if you are introducing a new dog to the household. Jealousy can be a major factor and your established dogs should always get the same, if not more attention than the newcomers.

Pack status is all important to an Ausky and if he's the established dog, he should be getting everything before the newcomer including attention, treats, greetings and so forth. Do not make the mistake of doting over the new puppy while ignoring the established Ausky. This will lead to serious problems in the pack. It is your duty as the leader to handle each pack member in the order of their status in the pack. Newcomers should always be at the bottom of the totem pole no matter how cute and cuddly they are.

Keep in mind that as welcoming as a Husky can be of other dogs, an Australian Cattle Dog can be aggressive and dominant toward other dogs, so your Ausky will fall somewhere in between depending on which genes are more prevalent. Expect dogs to maneuver for their place in the pack, but don't let the maneuvering turn into dog fights. If they acknowledge you as pack leader, the odds of the latter are greatly reduced.

The Rewards of Owning an Ausky Dog

If you've got the dog training experience to overcome the challenges of owning an Ausky dog, you'll find him to be an incredibly loyal friend and fun companion. The Ausky is what you'd call an all-terrain dog with built-in four wheel drive. He's a rugged, rough and tumble dog who is perfect for outdoor dog sports such as bikejoring, mushing, skijoring, canicross, carting, disc dog, flyball, herding, lure coursing, weight pulling, sled racing, and other high energy activities. He's got the stamina and endurance to join you for jogging, hiking, bicycling, and cross-country running. If you enjoy the challenge of creating games to make him think, you'll be amazed at his intelligence. Above all, he's quite a ham and he'll look for ways to tickle your funny bone. The challenges of owning an Ausky are manyfold, but the joys of befriending an Ausky will reward you for many years.

Deadly Prey

Dogs will eat anything!
(Even if it kills them)

The thrill of the chase — even if your dog isn't the sort to chase a cat or a child, most dogs will go after smaller game including bugs and toads. In the wild, part of a dog's diet consists of insects and other animals, so it's in the nature of a dog to go after such creatures.

However, you cannot rely on your dog's natural instincts to protect him. Pups in the wild learn about the dangers of nature from their mother. Domesticated dogs don't learn such things and can die from what seems to be an innocent pursuit. Dakota was notorious for such pursuits.

It was a warm, summer night in Georgia. Frogs were calling out for their mates, and cricket song filled the air. The moon was just a sliver in the sky and an owl hooted off in the distance.

I leaned on the railing gazing upward as Dakota disappeared into the blackness for her bedtime potty. The sky was full of stars and the music of the night creatures was a symphony of joy. All the world was happy.

My peaceful bliss quickly evaporated when Dakota came bounding up the stairs in frantic agitation. She was foaming at the mouth with long threads of goo flapping as she shook her head in panic, trying to rid herself of... what? She was pawing at her mouth. Foamy spittle was flying everywhere. What had she gotten into?

My mind raced through the possibilities. Some sort of poison? Our yard was fenced and there wasn't any poison for her to get into. Had someone thrown something over the fence? Dakota was an indoor dog so there was no barking to disturb the neighbors, no reason why anyone would want to harm her. Had she eaten a poisonous plant? Doom filled my belly as the prospect of her sudden death became very real. I panicked.

Should I give her something to make her vomit? Oh lordy I'd read so many books, I should *know* what would make her throw up. Come on, think! Hurry up and think! Urgent! Do something or she's going to die right here in your arms!

Tears came streaming down my face as I screamed for my husband, not knowing what to do for her. I loved her so much I couldn't bear to lose her. She wasn't even two years old. We should have at least a decade or more together. Oh Dakota... my beloved Dakota...

Something pulled me out of my panic — a glimpse of something, a clue, was she having trouble breathing? Maybe something was stuck in her throat?

I reached inside her mouth and felt around and sure enough, there was a smooth, round object lodged in her throat. What the...? Then it hit me. Our yard was full of toads, especially at night, and Dakota enjoyed chasing after them. Maybe she'd swallowed a toad and it got stuck in her throat.

With my whole hand in her mouth, I felt around hoping to grab a leg to pull it out, but all I could feel was a smooth, slimy surface that I couldn't get ahold of. I must have pushed it farther down because she gave a big swallow and it disappeared. The foam stopped. Her agitation calmed and suddenly she was my happy, healthy dog again.

We were lucky. Some toads are extremely poisonous and dogs die every year from eating them. The Sonoran Desert Toad (*Bufo alvarius*) and the southern Cane Toad (*Bufo marinus*) are two toxic toads. The Sonoran Desert Toad is found in southern California, Arizona, and New Mexico, while the Cane Toad is found primarily in Texas, Florida, and Hawaii. Other toads are not as toxic but all toads are poisonous to some degree. The Sonoran Desert Toad is so toxic that it can poison your dog simply by sitting in his water bowl.

Bufo marinus - CANE TOAD[1]

Toads release a toxin through their skin when they are threatened. A toad-poisoned dog will shake his head, drool, paw at his mouth and vomit. He may also have seizures or a heart attack depending on the toxicity of the toad.

If you believe that your dog has eaten or mouthed a toad, rinse his mouth with water from a hose and make sure that your

---

[1] This image is published under a Creative Commons Attribution-Share Alike 2.5 Generic license, courtesy of Jean-Marc Hero

dog does *not* swallow the water. This will help flush out some of the toad poison. Regardless, you should call your vet immediately.

The moral of the story is to prevent your dog from contact with toads if at all possible. Try to teach your dog to avoid toads. Do not encourage your dog to play with toads. What appears fun in the moment could be deadly for your dog.

Poison Candy

Even when you trust them...
(Don't!)

Dakota wasn't a dainty dog — she was a dog's dog and she was constantly flirting with death. Once again she put the fear of her death into me. First it was the hoof incident, then the toad incident, and now this.

We'd opened a bag of miniature chocolate candy bars the night before, eaten a couple and left the nearly full bag lying on the coffee table. Dakota was usually so good that we didn't even give it a second thought. She wasn't a trash digger and she wasn't in the habit of grabbing things off of tables, but just as with a child there will always be an exception.

She did the dirty deed just before breakfast. We found the empty bag of chocolates on the floor with the evidence scattered nearby. She'd eaten the candy bars wrappers and all, even the foils and papers were gone. All that was left was the empty bag, a couple of untouched chocolates, and one chocolate that she hadn't finished eating.

I'd always heard that chocolate was bad for dogs but now I needed to know how bad. Dakota had eaten so much — nearly a whole bag. I immediately researched chocolate and dogs on the internet and panicked when I found out how toxic it could be. Vomiting and diarrhea I could handle, but coma and death?

Internet veterinary sites offered calculations of toxic quantities but I was taking no chances — I called the vet. Even our veterinarian could not give us a definitive answer as to whether Dakota had eaten enough to need emergency care. He gave us the number of an emergency veterinary hospital that was more equipped for an emergency of this nature. They were an hour's drive away from us and my panic level shot through the roof. Did we have enough time to get her there if need be?

We told the emergency vet how many pounds she weighed and how much chocolate she'd eaten. Thank god we were able to give them specific information, especially on the type of chocolate and quantity eaten. Apparently there's a big difference in the toxicity of dark chocolate versus milk chocolate versus Baker's chocolate, and she had eaten mostly milk chocolate, the least toxic of the three.

The toxic ingredient is a stimulant called Theobromine, which is found in the cocoa plant. Stimulants affect the nervous system, cardiovascular system, and peripheral nerves. Symptoms include vomiting, diarrhea, restlessness, excitability, irritability, increased urination, rapid heartbeat, muscle tremors, and in high enough doses, coma and death. What we were facing was literally a drug overdose.

Semi-sweet dark chocolate is three times more toxic than milk chocolate, while Baker's chocolate is nine times more toxic. That means that a two ounce piece of Baker's chocolate is the toxic equivalent of eighteen ounces of milk chocolate.

The size of the dog, quantity of chocolate eaten, and most importantly the type of chocolate are the determining factors for the risk. Emergency veterinarians have special dosage calculators and if you know what and how much your dog ate, they can determine whether your dog should see a vet, be hospitalized, or is at low enough risk to stay home and ride it out.

It may take a few hours for symptoms to appear such as vomiting, diarrhea, restlessness, and hyperactivity. As the chocolate is digested and more of the toxin enters the bloodstream, your dog might experience rapid or irregular heartbeat, muscle twitching, heavy panting, and increased urination. In severe cases it can lead to elevated body temperature, muscle tremors, seizures, coma, and death.

If nobody knows how much the dog ate and there's a possibility that it was enough to be toxic, a vet will want to induce vomiting as soon as possible. Activated charcoal might prevent absorption of the toxins, and anticonvulsants may be used as well. Oxygen therapy, intravenous medications and fluids might be needed to protect the dog's heart.

In mild cases your dog might only suffer diarrhea and vomiting for up to 72 hours, and some dogs are more prone to the toxin than others. Old or sick dogs aren't as robust and will be more affected. Your safest course of action is to call an emergency vet or dog poison control center for professional advice. They can tell you what action to take and whether you should take your dog to the vet.

Dakota definitely put the fear of her death into me that night. Part of me wanted to reprimand her for doing something dangerously bad, and the other part was more focused on watching for symptoms and danger signs. Even though the vet said that she could stay home and ride it out, still it was prudent to keep an eye on her just in case her symptoms took a more dangerous turn.

We were lucky. Dakota progressed through symptoms including severe hyperactivity (as in bouncing off the walls, us, and anything else in her path), excessive thirst, and bright red gums. You can bet that we won't be leaving any more edibles on the coffee table or anywhere within her reach, especially those which might be toxic to dogs. Even for the most trustworthy dog, it's just not worth the risk.

BAD DOG TO BEST FRIEND

If your dog eats chocolate and shows signs of toxicity, he may need to be hospitalized so that supportive therapy can be given. For instance, if he is having seizures he may need anticonvulsive medications. The length of the hospitalization will depend on how much chocolate he ate and the severity of the symptoms. Usually he will be kept until the Theobromine has left his system.

Theobromine has a half life of seven hours. That means that in seven hours from the time your dog eats the chocolate, half of the Theobromine will have left his system. In another seven hours, half of that will be gone, and so on. Symptoms can last for up to 72 hours.

Stinky Dog

What's that awful smell?
(And why is it emanating from our dog?)

Not only do dogs eat whatever they can sink their teeth into, they roll in it. No matter how well-trained your dog is, don't forget that he's still a dog and that the natural behavior of a dog will curdle your stomach into a disgusted knot.

Dakota came into the house stinking like a dead thing. She'd only been outdoors a few minutes and in that short time, she'd gotten into something so foul smelling that you could smell her from several feet away. The whole room reeked of the smell of death, and all I could think of was that Dakota had found a dead animal and rolled on it.

Dogs roll on dead things to mask their own scent for when they're hunting. It's said that a dog rolling on dead animals is a throwback to their wild dog ancestry. When dogs hunt animals for food it helps if the prey can't smell the dog coming. Dakota definitely liked to roll on dead things. Even a dead bug would send her into a frenzy of orgasmic rolling.

It's easy for a dog to get covered in whatever stinky thing they find. Dakota is a house dog. She sleeps in the bedroom with us and spends most of her time indoors. Whatever she gets into outdoors, she joyfully brings in to share it with us. Lovelies such as poison ivy and even the turtle she brought in one day are a few of the joys of sharing your home with a dog.

DAKOTA ROLLING ON A DEAD BUG

Whatever she'd gotten into this time, the stench was horrible and poor Dakota couldn't understand why we were avoiding her. She smelled like a dead, rotting animal carcass and I figured if she'd rolled on a dead animal she'd surely be covered with nasty germs and bacteria. In just a matter of minutes, our dog had become a pariah dog — untouchable.

It was too late in the evening for a real dog bath and I was desperate. The thought of spending the night trying to sleep with this disgusting smell pervading the bedroom literally turned my stomach sour. I took a wet washcloth and gave Dakota a rub down with it, rinsing the washcloth and rubbing her fur again and again as I sniffed her coat to gauge my progress. You just can't have an indoor dog smelling like a rotting carcass.

I rubbed her vigorously all over concentrating on her back, shoulders, flanks, and scruff. Apparently I got most of it because there was just the tiniest whiff of a smell when I finished. The next morning I went in search of the dead thing in hopes of deleting it, but I couldn't find it. Try as I might, I could find no sign of a rotting carcass. I did find what appeared to be a stinky, rotting mushroom that looked like old dog poo, but that was about it.

The next day a full dog bath with plenty of shampoo washed the remnants of the bad smell away and Dakota was touchable again. Two days later I had a flash of inspiration as to the source of Dakota's smell. Rotting dead bodies weren't the only stinky things she could have rolled on.

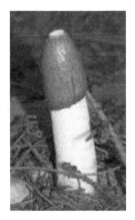

Phallus impudicus
STINKHORN MUSHROOM[2]

I'd been researching mushrooms for an article, and remembered reading about a mushroom called a Stinkhorn. I thought it was a longshot but worth a look, and discovered a bizarre mushroom in the process. Stinkhorn mushrooms come in a variety of strange shapes and just as I suspected, they stink beyond anything you could ever imagine.

---

[2] This image is published under a Creative Commons Attribution-Share Alike 3.0 Unported license, courtesy of Jean-Pol Grandmont

The scientific name for one variety of Stinkhorns is *Phallus impudicus* — and for good reason. They emerge from the ground looking much like a male sex organ — so much so that in the 1800s, Charles Darwin's daughter Henrietta "Etty" Darwin embarked on a mission to rid the world of what she considered to be the immoral Stinkhorn mushroom. Unlike her father in his quest to expose evolution, Etty preferred to burn the seedier aspects of it and set out on her own version of the Stinkhorn witch hunts.

Mutinus caninus
DOG STINKHORN MUSHROOM[3]

According to her niece Gwen in a memoir called *Period Piece*, Etty claimed to be the inventor of a sport whose goal it was to eradicate a toadstool called the Stinkhorn, whose scent was so powerful that you could hunt it by smell alone. Armed with a basket and pointed stick, Etty would hunt down Stinkhorns and using her pointed stick, *"poke his putrid carcase into her basket"*, later burning the toadstools *"in the deepest secrecy on the drawing-room fire, with the door locked; because of the morals of the maids."* (Gwen Raverat, Period Piece: Ann Arbor Paperbacks, 1976)

---

[3] This image is published under a Creative Commons Attribution-Share Alike 3.0 Unported license, courtesy of Roberto Zanon

Clathrus archeri - OCTOPUS STINKHORN MUSHROOM [4]

There are several varieties of Stinkhorns including the Octopus Stinkhorn, Devil's Fingers Stinkhorn, Chambered Stinkhorn, Stalked Lattice Stinkhorn, Columned Stinkhorn, Basket Fungus, Bamboo Fungus, Veiled Stinkhorn, Netted Stinkhorn, Common Stinkhorn, and Dog Stinkhorn. One of their claims to fame is that yes, they do stink. You can actually smell a Stinkhorn from quite a distance and they smell like either a pile of dog poop, raw sewage, or a dead animal.

Stinkhorns erupt from the ground as an egg-shaped mushroom and can grow several inches in a matter of hours. In the egg stage they are actually edible and some folks consider them quite a delicacy. All varieties share this innocent beginning

---

but they soon diversify into entities resembling a starfish, octopus, sex organ, Wiffle ball, or pretzel.

Lysurus periphragmoides
STALKED LATTICE STINKHORN COVERED WITH FLIES[5]

No matter what strange creature they resemble, sooner or later they will do what they do best — they will STINK. These mushrooms will emit a smell so overpowering that you could clear a room with a single Stinkhorn mushroom. That's how a Stinkhorn propagates. It emits a slimy, foul-smelling substance designed to attract flies. What self-deserving fly wouldn't zero in on a dead carcass or dog poop? The flies come sniffing around, the Stinkhorn spores stick to their feet, and the flies carry the spores off to multiply elsewhere making the Stinkhorn a pretty ingenious mushroom.

---

[5] This image is published under a Creative Commons Attribution-Share Alike 3.0 Unported license, courtesy of Steve Doonan

Dogs Will Be Dogs

How to teach your dog to ignore you
(You will make mistakes)

We may have had Stinkhorns growing in the yard attracting flies, but we were never bothered by flies in the house. Gypsy Rose could catch a fly in midair. Catching bugs, especially flying bugs, was one of her favorite pastimes, and this included wasps.

The first time Gypsy Rose tried to catch a wasp I stopped her, afraid that she would get stung. Hovering like an overprotective mother I would intervene. Wasps in the house were an uncommon occurrence so I didn't expect to encounter this issue again. I was in for quite a surprise.

The next day brought more wasps. So did the day after and many days to follow. The wasps kept coming. Apparently they had some secret door into the house.

Gypsy Rose was mesmerized by these loud, buzzing creatures. Flies had always been a favorite treat and the wasps were bigger and noisier. She yearned for the hunt and I was growing tired of being the bad guy who kept spoiling her joy, so one day I decided to just let her do what she wanted to do. I figured that Gypsy Rose would get stung and she'd learn not to mess with wasps again, and that would be the end of it.

To my utter disbelief she caught the wasp in mid-flight, pulling her lips back away from her teeth to snap the wasp in half. Several quick snaps of her teeth chopped the wasp to pieces before it could extend its stinger and the pieces disappeared down her throat as happy little dog treats. I was in awe — surely this was a fluke.

The days passed and Gypsy Rose caught wasp after wasp, thoroughly enjoying this tasty new morsel. I developed a morbid fascination in watching her accomplish this daring deed. If she got stung it did not faze her because for all the rest of her years, Gypsy Rose happily caught wasps and ate them. Gypsy Rose was our bug catcher.

Dakota preferred much bigger game. Being an Australian Cattle Dog/Siberian Husky mix, she was created of two dog breeds from some of the wildest, untamed territories known to man, and neither was a dainty breed.

While Dakota would happily tackle a bug on the floor and eat it, she did not master the art of catching flies in midair as Gypsy Rose had done. She much preferred the chase of small animals such as squirrels or chipmunks — a pursuit that fed her need to run fast and hard in the great outdoors.

Once outside it was a challenge to get Dakota to come back in. The call of the wild was an aphrodisiac full of irresistible temptations. Although she was a house dog, Dakota loved being outdoors. The treats I offered to lure her back inside paled in comparison to the wonders that Mother Nature had to offer.

One particular morning I let her out in the back yard for her final morning potty — the potty that would hold Dakota while we were at work. I let her have a few extra minutes outdoors while I prepared my lunch. When I called her to come back in, I was answered with silence. Something had captured her attention again.

I was about to go out after her when she finally came trotting up the stairs carrying something in her mouth. To my great surprise Dakota laid a four inch round turtle on the floor at my feet, her eyes shining with pure joy. The turtle was tucked tight into his shell and appeared to be unharmed.

"Look at the really cool thing I found in the woods!" her eyes seemed to say. *"Can I have it please? Can I keep it?"* Joy and innocence shined in her eyes as she shared this great moment with me.

Being more focused on getting to work, I didn't stop to think how I should handle this important moment in our dog's life. I picked up the turtle and gently told her no, she could not have the turtle, and then I took it outdoors and let it go free and off to work I went.

The event haunted me. I'd missed a golden opportunity. I got halfway up the street when I had to turn around. All I could think about was how I should have taken pictures of Dakota and the turtle before taking it away. I should have taken a picture of the turtle up next to something to demonstrate its size. I should have taken a photo of Dakota's happy face, of her holding the turtle, of the turtle on the ground at her feet. I should have preserved this special moment to remember it always. This was an important moment for Dakota — sharing this big find. I had to go back. I had to take pictures.

I turned the car around and went back home with the intention of bringing the turtle back in for a couple of quick photos and then setting it loose again. A five minute delay — that's all I needed — but there was one dilemma: the turtle was gone. I searched high and low for that turtle, all through the woods and across the yard, circling wider and wider. Surely he couldn't have disappeared so quickly? How far could a turtle have possibly gotten? I searched and searched to no avail. The turtle was nowhere to be found. He wanted no part of us and who could blame him?

All the way to work I tormented myself over an additional mistake I'd made in reacting to Dakota with the turtle. I realized

169

that I'd handled the whole affair totally wrong. Dakota had brought that turtle to me having no idea that I'd take it away from her. Now she'd never attempt to bring another turtle in. From that moment forward she simply wouldn't come when I called her. I'd worked so hard in trying to train her to come in when I called and now I'd sent the message loud and clear that to keep her tasty dog treat, she'd have to stay outdoors and ignore my calls. We'd been struggling with this stage of her dog training and I had totally blown it.

What should I have done? I believe I should have given her something in trade. The moment I took the turtle away I should have given her a highly desirable dog treat in its place. That's how we taught her what she could chew in the house — we traded legal dog chews for illegal objects.

The tactic had worked well and Dakota had learned not to chew anything except what we gave her to chew. Rather than focusing totally on the negative, the *no*, we were swapping it with a positive. We didn't just punish her by taking something away and leaving her frustrated. We offered a replacement to entice her to make a good decision.

The trade for the turtle should have been a biggie, too, not just a measly dog biscuit. Peanut butter, a piece of meat, or an expensive dog treat would have been good choices. Had I traded for the turtle I would have sent the message that the turtle was not okay without frustrating her. Instead, I had sent the message that she'd better go find a hidey hole if she wanted to keep her turtles. If mama calls you'd better run and hide!

Dakota's First Road Trip

Dakota's first adventure
(We're going on a road trip!)

For all of the activities that we couldn't let her do, and all of the tidbits we couldn't let her have, we made up for it in other ways. Once we'd tackled Dakota's serious issues and were confident in her ability to stay home alone, the next step was to take her to somebody else's house.

There is hope for even the most godawful dog. Dakota is living proof of that. She came to us as the most godawful dog you could ever imagine, and for the celebration of her one year anniversary with us, we were taking her on a road trip.

We knew from our trial runs and trips to the vet that she was deathly afraid of going into the truck. Rides for Dakota had always meant abandonment or a bad boarding experience. Car rides had never meant anything good.

The prospect of trusting Dakota loose in the back seat of the truck filled me with angst. The thought of taking Dakota to someone else's house was even worse. While she had made tremendous improvements over the past year, I did not trust her one hundred percent. Memories of her godawful behavior in the beginning were still very fresh.

We took the dog crate with us, totally expecting her to spend the entire vacation in it. After her bad boarding experience we felt she was better off to spend several days in her familiar crate with us nearby, than to go to a kennel again. We made it clear to our friends that we were willing to keep her in the crate if need be, as we did not want them worrying about their house. Hope for the best but prepare for the worst.

The Arsenal
(We were prepared for anything)

We brought along the buzz collar, dog harness, several old blankets and towels in case she peed or vomited in the truck, and a bag of raw baby carrots for bribery. Dakota loved raw carrots.

We debated a long time on how to travel with her. The back seat of the truck folded down flat, and Gypsy Rose had always traveled loose in the back seat. Did we dare try it with Dakota? Would she go crazy and jump around, dangerously distracting the driver? Would she stress out and pee? Should we put the crate in the back seat with both dogs in it?

When we first purchased the crate, we chose the biggest one they made that would fit in the back seat of the truck, specifically to allow us to travel with both dogs crated. This particular crate folded up like a suitcase. In order to get it in the truck we had to put it in the back seat folded up, and then unfold it. Once fully opened, the crate took up the entire back seat with no room to spare. It had a door at each end to let the dogs out during pit stops. That was the original plan.

However, the plastic bottom caused both dogs to slide around and when we tried taking the bottom out it left the uncomfortable grille of the cage exposed. We could have piled it up with blankets but we were still debating on whether to leave the dogs loose. It was so hard to trust Dakota — especially with her mortal fear of being in the truck.

Dare we risk it? Can she handle the freedom?
(Or play it safe and suck all their joy away)

Being in the crate would really demote the travel experience for both dogs, but it would be much safer. All of the dog experts recommend confinement for both the safety of the dog and the driver. Would Dakota go bonkers and ricochet around the truck if left loose? We had no idea what to expect but ever optimistic, we decided to try leaving both dogs loose and if we needed to pull over and set up the crate, we would.

Dakota did *not* want to go into the truck. The first thing she did when we tried to pick her up was pee on the driveway. It was definitely a stress pee and it was not a good sign. All four feet splayed outward and stiffened in an attempt to prevent being shoved into the truck, Dakota fought hard. She didn't wanna. She was in full panic and we could not allay her fears. Even though we'd taken her on two short fun rides earlier in the week she was not convinced. Rides were bad. Rides meant abandonment. Owners took her for a ride and she never saw them again. Dakota was deathly afraid.

Please don't pee in the truck! Or worse, lay in it after...
(A pee stinky dog would be godawful to travel with)

We had lined the truck seat with several thick blankets and a piece of thick carpeting in case Dakota let loose. Sooner or later you have to take a risk. Finally we got both dogs bundled into the back seat and we set off on a thirteen hour road trip. That's a lot of hours for a fearful dog who doesn't know what to expect. It was a brave move for us to take with her.

Dakota was on her feet for the entire thirteen hours — stiff legged in full panic and breathing hard with a look of sheer torment on her face. There was nothing we could do but keep on driving. We stopped several times extra to let her out to pee and every time, she'd fight like the dickens to avoid going back in the

173

truck. Poor Gypsy Rose didn't get a moment's rest because Dakota was on her feet the entire trip.

Are we there yet?
(Yup, now what's she gonna do?)

We finally arrived at our destination — now what? How would Dakota react to being in a stranger's house with us? We were staying with friends. Would she immediately pee on their rug? Could we trust her loose at night in the bedroom like we did at home? Could we trust her to be in the house at all, knowing that getting her from the crate to the potty spot could be fraught with danger for the carpet? We had no idea what these changes would do to Dakota or how it would affect her training. Would all of her training fly out the window?

We arrived just in time for bed. Our friends were already in bed so we tried to be as quiet as we possibly could. We tiptoed in and out with our luggage. It was impossible to spend time with Dakota to acclimate her after our arrival. Outside it was too dark to even choose a good pee spot for her. I would have liked to have had fun time with Dakota to let her wind down and relax but there wasn't much I could do. It was bedtime and we didn't want to disturb our hosts.

Again, we opted for giving Dakota a chance and we all piled into the bedroom, two humans and two dogs. Dakota's crate was set up in case we needed it and all of our suitcases were piled around the room. We went to bed just like at home with both dogs loose in the bedroom, and though she was still on edge, Dakota slept quietly just like at home.

Day One - Dakota goes to the beach!
(All of her worries wash away)

The first thing we did after breakfast was take the dogs to the beach. We were on the ocean in the Outer Banks of North

Carolina, a beautiful place where the beach stretches for miles. Much of the Outer Banks is a nature preserve and totally unspoiled. There were no hotels for miles around — just private rentals and residences.

DAKOTA CHECKS OUT THE OCEAN

We were in Rodanthe, the very place the book *Nights in Rodanthe* was written about. Several of the beach house rentals in Rodanthe are dog-friendly but we weren't at a rental, we stayed with friends about five houses back from the beach.

Dakota woke up stressed and agitated. She was still worried that this was another abandonment. We put a harness on her and off we went to gallivant by the ocean. We took her right to the edge of the ocean where the water could splash on her feet. Dakota was perplexed. This was not what she expected.

Dakota was with us, her family, in an exciting new environment. There wasn't a dog kennel or dog pound in sight and she finally relaxed and embraced the moment. She walked slowly at first in the shifting sand with the water splashing at her legs. We made a big game of everything to send the message that we were here for *fun*.

DAKOTA FINALLY REALIZES THAT WE'RE HERE FOR FUN

Before long Dakota was charging into the waves with gusto letting them wash her back to shore. I had ahold of her by harness and leash and knew that she was safe in my control.

Dakota had a blast. All of the worry and fear washed away from her and she fully embraced this strange new adventure, frolicking and splashing in the big waves and drinking the salty water. Her eyes shined with joy and wonder as we walked down the beach, soaking in strange new sights and sounds and smells.

New things were everywhere. There were people and other dogs and seagulls skittering across the sand. Strange smells came in on the ocean breeze and everything was a great adventure, a new world to explore. Dakota danced and pranced and sniffed the wet sand and came nose to nose with a giant crab. It reared up on its hind legs and pointed its big claw at her in warning. They faced off for a few moments, eyeing each other in a silent stare before I tugged her leash and we went on our merry way. Dakota was having the time of her life.

Five gold stars for Dakota!
(She's well on her way to being the Perfect Dog)

From that moment forward all the fear washed away and she embraced this new thing we were doing. We spent two full days in the Outer Banks and Dakota was a model citizen. She was so well behaved that our friends could not believe that we'd even had a fear. We hadn't once raided the arsenal we'd brought with us. Dakota spent the whole trip on nothing more than a leash and ordinary harness.

She quickly learned the new potty routine, food routine, and bedtime routine. Not a bark came out of her, not a bad pee pee, not a single moment of disobedience. Dakota was for those days, the perfect dog and the perfect canine guest. We were amazed — absolutely and utterly amazed. We knew we'd worked hard with her for a whole year but you could not call her a perfect model citizen at home. Knowing how afraid she was of change we had fully expected the absolute worst.

All too quickly it was time for the thirteen hour ride back home. The morning started with Dakota in a panic about entering the truck but after that first hoist up, she settled down and slept all the way home with her head resting on the armrest between our seats. She needed to feel close to us. The trip had been a very big step for her.

The ride home went much smoother than the ride there. All the potty stops went quickly. She jumped out on her own, peed on command, and climbed back into the truck without assistance and without fear.

DAKOTA SLEEPS PEACEFULLY ALL THE WAY HOME

We had put all of the bad memories to rest for her. All of Dakota's abandonment fears washed far out into the ocean. Hopefully in the future she would embrace the truck as a vehicle for fun and adventure. What an incredibly good feeling it was to know that we had brought joy to a dog who started life joyless and unloved.

We were overjoyed to see the fruits of our very hard work in retraining her. The many months of frustration, the wondering if we'd done the right thing in adopting her, the torment our other dog went through, the torment that *we* went through, all of it washed away into the sands by the seashore.

178

IN TRAINING TO BE THE PERFECT DOG

69249700R00101

Made in the USA
Lexington, KY
27 October 2017